BLOOD FIRE
AND
Vapor of Smoke

BLOOD
FIRE
AND
Vapor of Smoke

by
Mark Brazee

MBM Publications
Broken Arrow, Oklahoma

Unless otherwise indicated all Scripture quotations are taken from the *King James Version* of the Bible.

Blood, Fire, and Vapor of Smoke
Third Printing 1998
ISBN 0-934445-06-0
Copyright © 1996 by Mark Brazee Ministries
P. O. Box 1870
Broken Arrow, Oklahoma 74013

Published by MBM Publications

Printed in the United States of America.

Table of Contents

Pg 58

Chapter 1
Holy Ghost Fire: God's Divine Sparkplug for Revival

In the Christian world today, a tremendous outpouring of the Holy Ghost is sweeping the Church. A common occurrence in these meetings is an outbreak of joy, Holy Ghost laughter, and dancing in the Spirit. Through these outpourings of joy, we have discovered that people's lives have been dramatically changed.

But meetings like these also stir up many questions, including: What is going on here? Is this God or just emotionalism? And if this is God, what is His purpose?

However, we need to realize that throughout history, revivals have often been accompanied by such unusual demonstrations. Could this be the beginning of revival? And if so, what are such outbreakings of the Holy Ghost supposed to accomplish?

As a teacher, I've been stirred to study God's Word, line upon line, regarding this new Pentecostal fire that is sweeping the world.

Mighty Demonstrations — God's Show!

Actually, when we look into God's Word, we can see that God predicted that certain signs and wonders would mark the end of the age.

ACTS 2:19,20
19 And I will shew WONDERS IN HEAVEN ABOVE, and SIGNS IN THE EARTH beneath; BLOOD, and FIRE, and VAPOUR OF SMOKE. 20 The sun shall be turned into darkness, and the moon into blood, before that great and notable day of the Lord come.

God is talking about two major demonstrations of power: Wonders in the heavens and signs on the Earth. God didn't tell us what all of the wonders and signs would be, for there will be many amazing manifestations of God's power. But He did give us two examples. He said that in the *heavens*, the sun would be turned to darkness and the moon to blood. And on the *Earth*, there would be blood, fire, and vapor of smoke. In studying this verse, I found that most commentaries say this verse refers to war, destruction, murder, burning buildings, and cities on fire.

But God said, *"I will show."* God wants to put on a show! Burning cities is not God's idea of putting on a show. People being murdered and killed is not God's idea of putting on a show. When God puts on a show, it's not to destroy man but to show man that He is God. He is talking about putting on a show of Holy Ghost signs and wonders. Miraculous signs and wonders are always supernatural manifestations of the Holy Ghost. So if these signs don't refer to war and destruction, what exactly do they refer to?

The Blood

When God speaks about blood, He's not talking about man's blood, but a higher kind of blood — the supernatural blood of Jesus (Matthew 26:28). By blood, God is talking about the plan of redemption — what has been bought and paid for through the death, burial, and resurrection of Jesus. When a life is changed, born again, or healed by the power of the shed blood of Jesus, that's a sign.

The Smoke

Then what is the smoke? Smoke refers to that same pillar of smoke that rested over the tent of the testimony in the Old Testament (Numbers 9:15). The vapor of smoke doesn't refer to buildings burning, but rather to supernatural smoke — the glory of God — the manifested presence of God. Often in the Old Testament the glory cloud of God appeared like a smoke or a cloud (Isaiah 4:5; Isaiah 6:4; Exodus 13:21,22; Exodus 40:34).

The Fire

So we understand what the blood and the vapor of smoke refer to. But what about the fire? What kind of fire is God talking about? It is the same supernatural fire that fell on the Day of Pentecost when there appeared unto believers "...Cloven tongues like as of FIRE.... And they were all filled with the HOLY GHOST... (Acts 2:3,4). The fire refers to the fire of God — the Holy Ghost.

John the Baptist also referred to the fire of God. Notice that the *fire* accompanies the baptism in the Holy Ghost.

> **LUKE 3:16,17**
> **16 John answered, saying unto them all, I indeed baptize you with water; but one mightier than I cometh, the latchet of whose shoes I am not worthy to unloose: he shall baptize you with THE HOLY GHOST and with FIRE:**
> **17 Whose fan is in his hand, and he will thoroughly purge his floor, and will gather the wheat into his garner; but the chaff HE WILL BURN WITH FIRE unquenchable.**

Actually, John the Baptist was looking into the future when he said this. He was seeing the day of the New Covenant when Jesus would baptize believers with the Holy Ghost and fire. John was referring to what would happen on the Day of Pentecost.

The Fire of God Burns Off the Chaff

So the blood of Jesus redeems us, and the glory of God brings in the miraculous, but what is the fire for? John the Baptist said in Luke 3:16,17, "...He shall baptize you with the Holy Ghost and with fire: Whose fan is in his hand, and he will thoroughly purge his floor, and will gather the wheat into his garner; but the chaff he will burn with fire unquenchable."

In the Old Testament, a fan was an instrument like a pitchfork that was used to throw the wheat into the air. The wind separated and blew the chaff away so the wheat could fall back to the ground pure. They would then put the wheat in the barn and burn the chaff.

John the Baptist was saying that the day was coming when the anointing or fire of God would separate the wheat from the chaff so our lives could be pure before God. The fire of God refines us. It burns off all the chaff and gets us ready for the glory.

In the natural, farmers burn the chaff and keep the wheat. That's what God wants to do in our lives — burn off the chaff, the "excess baggage," so we can get over into the glory.

By chaff or excess baggage, we don't mean outward sins like smoking, drinking, or immorality, although people have been delivered from these bondages by the manifested presence of God. But there is more chaff that needs to be burned off the Body of Christ than just sin.

God wants to burn off anything that holds us back from doing His will — whether it's oppression, depression, sickness, or disease. In the Bible, God calls those "weights." Weights slow us down in our spiritual walk so it's hard to make any progress.

HEBREWS 12:1
1 Wherefore seeing we also are compassed about with so great a cloud of witnesses, let us lay aside EVERY WEIGHT, and the sin which doth so easily beset us, and let us run with patience the race that is set before us....

The fire of God burns off any weights, including anything that would hold us back in our spiritual race.

So the blood of Jesus brings us into the family of God, but we have to go through the fire to be prepared for His glory. We can preach and teach on the glory, and the glory of God will manifest. But we are not going to enter into the fullness of the glory of God until He gets us ready for it by the fire of God.

I have heard people say when their lives are full of tests, trials, and tribulations that they are experiencing a baptism of fire. No, the fire of God doesn't *give* us tests, trials, and tribulations; it *burns them off* of us. The fire is not a judgment to weigh us down; it is the power of the Holy Ghost to set us free.

The Fire of God Changes People

The fire of God changes us so God can use us to His glory. Peter is a good example of someone who was changed by the fire of God. He was the best disciple Jesus had: the best trained, the most mature, and the most dependable, yet Peter denied Jesus three times. Why? He was too timid to witness. He needed some chaff burned off. When the Holy Ghost and fire came into that Upper Room, it changed Peter's life. After that he went into the streets and boldly preached the Gospel.

On the Day of Pentecost when the fire of God fell and believers spoke in tongues, the devout Jews stood up and said, "What does this mean?" (Acts 2:12).

Peter said, "I'll tell you what this means: These people are not drunk, but this is the outpouring that you have been looking for. You just didn't recognize it." Then he preached about the death, burial, and resurrection of Jesus, and 3000 people were born again in his first altar call (Acts 2:41). The fire of

God transformed Peter from a spiritual weakling to a powerful preacher.

The Fire Changes the Course of a Life

Moses was another person who was dramatically changed by the fire of God. In fact, the whole course of his life was changed when he came into contact with God's fire.

When Moses was in Egypt, it came into his heart to be a deliverer of his people. But he tried to do it in his own strength and killed a man. Moses ran for his life and spent 40 years in the desert. He was on the backside of the desert when the angel of the Lord appeared to him in a flame of fire out of the midst of a burning bush.

> **EXODUS 3:1,2**
> **1 Now Moses kept the flock of Jethro his father in law, the priest of Midian: and he led the flock to the backside of the desert, and came to the mountain of God, even to Horeb.**
> **2 And the angel of the Lord appeared unto him IN A FLAME OF FIRE out of the midst of a bush: and he looked, and, behold, THE BUSH BURNED WITH FIRE, and the bush was not consumed.**

When Moses came into contact with the fire of God, it changed the course of his life. God equipped him with signs, wonders, and miracles and said, "You tried to be a deliverer of your people before, but now I am sending you to be a ruler and deliverer of *My* people."

God sent Moses back to Egypt a changed man. After his encounter with the fire of God, Moses, who was now powerfully anointed by God, brought approximately 3 million Jews out of bondage into freedom. It was the fire of God that changed Moses from a shepherd on the backside of the desert to a deliverer of a nation.

The Fire of God Will Change a Ministry

The fire of God can also change the course of a person's ministry. That's what happened to Elisha. In First Kings 19:16, God spoke to Elijah and said, "Go anoint Elisha son of Shaphat to take your place."

So Elijah found Elisha and cast his mantle upon him. You see, in the Old Testament, a "mantle" was an outer cloak or garment that was symbolic of the prophet's anointing. Elisha left his business and started following Elijah. Elisha served Elijah in the ministry of helps for 11 to 15 years. But finally, it was time for Elijah to depart; his earthly ministry was complete. It was time for Elisha to take Elijah's place of anointing in the office of the prophet (2 Kings 2:8-14).

Elisha stayed close to Elijah day and night. Finally Elijah turned to Elisha and asked, "What do you want?"

Elisha answered, "I pray thee, let a double portion of thy spirit be upon me" (2 Kings 2:9). In this verse, the words "spirit" and "anointing" are synonymous terms. So when Elisha said, "I want a double portion of your spirit," or of the spirit that's upon you, he was really saying, "I want a double portion of the anointing that's on your life."

Now if Elisha had wanted a double portion of the anointing so he could become twice as famous, draw twice the crowds, or make twice as much money, he wouldn't have received it. God only answers prayers that are prayed from *pure* motives. Therefore, Elisha's motives must have been right because he received the double portion. Elisha knew the anointing destroys the yoke and sets the captives free, and his heart was to minister to people.

While Elisha was watching Elijah being caught away in the chariot of fire (2 Kings 2:11), Elijah's mantle came floating down from heaven. When that mantle fell, Elisha picked it up, and walked over to the Jordan River. Then he said, "Where is the Lord God of Elijah?"

He didn't ask where Elijah went; he didn't care. That's not what was important. He just wanted the Lord God of Elijah. He knew enough not to look to man but to look to God. He wrapped the mantle together, smote the waters, and they parted again. He walked across on dry ground.

When Elisha came in contact with the fire of God, it changed the course of his ministry. He received the double portion of Elijah's anointing. In fact, when you study Elisha's ministry, God wrought twice the miracles, signs and wonders through his ministry as He did in Elijah's.

So we can see that the fire of God accomplishes several things in the believer's life. The fire of God burns up the chaff — the excess baggage and the weights in the believer's life. In other words, it refines us; it burns off anything that would slow us down in our spiritual race. It gets us ready for the glory.

The fire of God also changes us. Just as in Peter's life, the fire can change us from being ordinary to being supernaturally empowered to accomplish God's plan and purpose. As with Moses, it can change the course of our lives. As with Elisha, the fire can change the course of our ministries. But the fire of God also gets us ready for the rain of the Holy Spirit. Let's back up and look at what happened in Elijah's ministry.

The Fire of God Will Change a Nation

In First Kings 17:1, Elijah prayed by the unction of the Holy Ghost, and it didn't rain for three and a half years. That's a drought! God supernaturally took care of Elijah as long as he followed the Holy Ghost and obeyed God. But then God spoke to him again (1 Kings 18:1) and said, "Go find Ahab and tell him you want to talk to him."

When Elijah found King Ahab, he told him, "You've been leading the nation astray. Go find the 450 prophets of Baal and the prophets of the groves, and bring them up here — we are going to have a showdown."

Then Elijah turned to the false prophets and said, "Now we are going to find out whose God answers by fire. You make your altar, put your sacrifice on it, call on your gods, and see what they can do."

The prophets of Baal made their altar and put their sacrifice on it, and all these false prophets began to cry out to their gods.

Elijah mocked them and said, "Cry a little louder; maybe he's on the telephone. Cry a little louder! He may be doing business in the back office, or maybe he's on vacation. Or maybe he's taking a nap."

Finally, Elijah said, "Get out of the way; it's my turn."

Elijah built an altar and put wood and sacrifice on it. But he wanted to make sure Baal's false prophets couldn't say that it was just spontaneous combustion. So he said, "Dig a trench and pour 12 barrels of water on it." They poured water until the sacrifice was soaked. The altar was so saturated that the water ran off the edge and completely filled the trench.

Then Elijah prayed, "God, send down Your fire. Let the people know I did this at Your Word." Elijah didn't cry and cut himself, moan, groan, or wail. No, he just said, "God, move!" And fire fell from heaven. When it did, the fire consumed the sacrifice, the wood, the altar, and all the water.

All the nation of Israel who were watching this showdown fell on their faces and said, "The Lord, he is the God" (1 Kings 18:39). These were the same people who, a few hours earlier, were wavering between God and the false god Baal. The fire fell and the whole nation fell on their face and worshiped God. The fire of God not only changed the entire nation of Israel, but it ushered in a reverence for God.

The Fire of God Brings the Rain of God

Notice that after the fire of God fell, the rain came. Elijah told Ahab, "...Get thee up, eat and drink; for there is a sound of abundance of rain" (1 Kings 18:41). That's how it is in the spiritual realm, too. After the fire falls, the next stage is the outpouring of the Holy Ghost. We are looking for the rain — the outpouring of the Holy Ghost. The greatest move of God this Earth has ever seen is about to be demonstrated. But before we get to the fullness of the rain of the Holy Ghost and the glory of God, we need an encounter with the fire of God.

God is changing people's callings; He is changing the direction of people's lives; He is burning off chaff; and He is getting rid of all the excess baggage. He is setting us free to run with the move of God.

The Fire of God Brings Enjoyable Change

God is a life-changing God, but He also understands man's nature. He knows that even in the natural, change is easier when it's more enjoyable.

For example, years ago my jaw began to hurt, so I went to the dentist. He told me I needed to have a wisdom tooth pulled. He said, "This tooth may only cause you a little trouble now, but if you don't have it removed, it will cause you even more trouble later." This dentist only gave me novocaine for the pain. It seemed like he just put his pliers in my mouth, placed one foot on my chest, and started pulling! When it was all over, I thought *I'm never going to go through this again! That was not enjoyable!*

Later, a different dentist told me that I needed to have another wisdom tooth pulled or it would cause me problems. So I asked, "Do you have anything that could make this experience more enjoyable?"

He said, "Yes, I use nitrous oxide or laughing gas. Extracting the tooth won't hurt you at all."

So I decided to let him pull my tooth. I thought, *Maybe this will be less uncomfortable.* I can still remember when the dentist gave me the first dose of nitrous oxide. He said, "Take a couple of breaths." Believe me — after the third breath, I was thoroughly enjoying myself!

After the tooth was extracted and the effects of the nitrous oxide were beginning to wear off, the dentist said, "This is really strange. Your X ray shows that not only do you have that one wisdom tooth, but there's another one growing right behind it. If I don't pull it now, it's going to give you trouble later."

At this point, I was feeling so good I said, "Take every tooth out of my mouth if you want, Doc. Pull anything — all of them! Just give me more of that laughing gas!"

I didn't feel a thing when those two wisdom teeth were extracted. I had a wonderful time. I felt so good, I wanted to take a can of that laughing gas home with me.

God is endeavoring to remove things out of our lives that at times could be painful to be removed. Some things may be causing trouble now, and if they are not removed, they will give us more trouble later. He wants us to get rid of our "excess baggage."

So what is God doing during these Holy Ghost meetings when the fire from heaven falls? God is giving us a good dose of "Holy Ghost nitrous oxide" — His kind of laughing gas!

When we are in services where we are laughing and having a wonderful time, we are on God's operating table. He's reaching down inside us and making adjustments. He's taking out things that are holding us back in our spiritual walk. We leave these services saying, "Oh, wasn't that wonderful?"

A week later we notice that something that was giving us pain or a problem in a certain area of our lives is completely gone! We didn't know how to get rid of it, but when we were on God's operating table, filled with His "Holy Ghost nitrous oxide," He pulled that pain, discomfort, and excess baggage out, and we never even felt a thing.

That's what God is doing in the Church right now. He's getting rid of excess baggage. He is saying, "I need to remove some things from your life, but I have an operating table that you are going to enjoy!" Then the Holy Ghost fills us up, and we say to God, "Take out anything you like!"

God is doing far more than we know during these Holy Ghost operations. He's making spiritual deposits and changing things in people's lives. He's making change enjoyable, because when people are full of the Holy Ghost, change doesn't hurt!

So God is releasing His Holy Ghost fire to burn the chaff and get rid of the excess baggage in our lives.

Baptized With the Holy Ghost and Fire

I used to think that when God spoke about fire, He was speaking about judgment. I imagined that

God was in heaven ready to hit us with a big baseball bat. But that picture is not consistent with Biblical accounts of the fire of God when it fell. Yes, there is a fire that pertains to judgment, but the Church isn't under God's wrath and judgment. There is another kind of fire that brings blessing and benefit to the Church. We can see an example of the fire of God as it pertains to the Church in the Book of Acts.

> **ACTS 2:1-4**
> **1 And when the Day of Pentecost was fully come, they were all with one accord in one place.**
> **2 And suddenly there came a sound from heaven as of a rushing mighty wind, and it filled all the house where they were sitting.**
> **3 And there appeared unto them cloven tongues like AS OF FIRE, and it sat upon each of them.**
> **4 And THEY WERE ALL FILLED WITH THE HOLY GHOST, and began to speak with other tongues, as the Spirit gave them utterance.**

When believers were baptized in the Holy Ghost, they were filled with the fire of God. What did the fire of God produce? Did it bring judgment? No! It filled the Church with Holy Ghost power, ability, and might (Acts 1:8 *The Amplified Bible*).

What kind of fire is this that is going to change the course of our lives and that is going to burn off the chaff? Is this a fire that will burn us up? No, it's fire that will set us free. It's the fire of the Holy Ghost.

Where is the fire? It's in believers! Notice that the fire of God filled believers on the *inside* and changed them on the *outside*. Most of us want changes to come from the outside first, but God always produces changes from the inside out. If we will get filled up with the fire of God, it will burn off the chaff from the inside out.

What is this move of God where people are so filled with joy and laughter, they get drunk in the Holy Ghost? *It's the fire of God!*

Thank God for the blood of the Lord Jesus Christ, for the vapor of smoke, and for the glory that brings manifestations of the Holy Ghost in signs, wonders, and miracles. But there's a step before we can get to the glory. We've come through the blood of Jesus, and we want to get to the glory, but we need to get filled with the fire of God first.

Chapter 2

A Holy Union:
The Word and Spirit

The fire is the outpouring of the Holy Ghost which often manifests itself in joy. If we are not careful, though, we can focus on what is happening on the outside and forget about what is going on inside. God is changing the Church from the inside out. And the fire is not just emotionalism — it is God using a combination of the Word and the Spirit to impart changes in us.

A good example of how God combines the Word and Spirit is found in Ezekiel 37, which describes a vision pertaining to the house of Israel. Often, scriptures can have a two- or three-fold application, even though this mainly pertains to Israel. Ezekiel's vision of the dry bones could also be a picture of the Church in the last days.

EZEKIEL 37:1-8
1 The hand of the Lord was upon me, and carried me out in the spirit of the Lord, and set me down in the midst of the valley which was full of bones,
2 And caused me to pass by them round about: and, behold, there were very many in the open valley; and, lo, they were very dry.
3 And he said unto me, Son of man, can these bones live? And I answered, O Lord God, thou knowest.
4 Again he said unto me, Prophesy upon these bones, and say unto them, O ye dry bones, hear the word of the Lord.

5 Thus saith the Lord God unto these bones; Behold, I will cause breath to enter into you, and ye shall live:
6 And I will lay sinews upon you, and will bring up flesh upon you, and cover you with skin, and put breath in you, and ye shall live; and ye shall know that I am the Lord.
7 So I prophesied as I was commanded: and as I prophesied, there was a noise, and behold a shaking, and the bones came together, bone to his bone.
8 And when I beheld, lo, the sinews and the flesh came up upon them, and the skin covered them above....

God spoke to Ezekiel in the valley full of dry bones, and Ezekiel began to speak the Word. When the Word went forth, skin and ligaments appeared, and the bones came together. Verse 10 says that a great army was formed.

This passage is also a picture of what God has done throughout past revivals. For years, people have been speaking the Word, and bones have been coming together. This great army, the Church, is being raised up. But it's not enough to do the work that God has planned for the Church. Look at verses 8 through 10:

EZEKIEL 37:8-10
8 ...but there was no breath in them.
9 Then said he unto me, Prophesy unto the wind, prophesy, son of man, and say to the wind, Thus saith the Lord God; Come from the four winds, O breath, and breathe upon these slain, that they may live.

10 So I prophesied as he commanded me, and the breath came into them, and they lived, and stood up upon their feet, an exceeding great army.

God knew the first thing He had to do was speak the Word to raise up the body, and get the bones, muscles, tendons and ligaments together to hold the body steady.

But that was not enough — there was another part. When God told Ezekiel to prophesy again, the wind blew. Suddenly there was a great living army. First Ezekiel prophesied, or spoke God's Word to the bones, and then the wind blew on them, and they became an exceeding great army.

I believe God is saying that the Church, the army of God, is ripe for the wind or breath of the Spirit. Faith, healing, prosperity, and good sound doctrines have been poured into the Church for years. A basic foundation has been laid which started bringing the bones, muscles, ligaments, and skin together. Now it's time for the wind to blow. We need a move of the Spirit of God.

Zechariah 4:6 says, "...Not by might, nor by power, but by my Spirit...." We need both the Word and the Spirit.

So now there is a great Body of Christ all over the world. But God is getting ready to breathe the wind of His Spirit on this great army. God has a plan, and it will come to pass; but God is a god of order, and it will happen His way.

How God Accomplishes
His Plan on This Earth

God has a plan for our lives, our families, our churches, our cities, the nations, and the world. But He doesn't just wing it and say, "I wonder what I'll do today?" God knows what He's doing. God has a plan, and it always comes to pass the same way.

In the book of beginnings, Genesis 1, God shows how He always accomplishes His plan on the Earth.

> **GENESIS 1:1-3**
> **1 In the beginning God created the heaven and the earth.**
> **2 And the earth was without form, and void; and darkness was upon the face of the deep. And the SPIRIT OF GOD MOVED upon the face of the waters.**
> **3 AND GOD SAID, Let there be light: and there was light.**

Notice that two things happened here. In verse 3, God said, "Let there be light." But something happened before He said that. Verse 2 says, "...the Spirit of God moved upon the face of the waters."

The first thing God showed us is that in order to accomplish what He wanted accomplished on the Earth it took two things: God spoke the Word, and the Holy Ghost moved.

When God said, "Let there be light," the Spirit of God, who was already moving, hooked up with and confirmed the Word with signs following, and then there was light. This is God's way: He speaks His Word, and the Spirit of God confirms the Word.

The move of the Holy Ghost is not some wild, emotional kind of move. It is God putting forth His Word and then confirming that Word with signs following. *Whatever Word we preach, God will confirm with signs following.* It's not that we don't have to have preaching and teaching anymore. No, we need a combination of the Word *and* the Spirit.

The way God is going to move is to send forth His Word along with an outpouring of the Holy Spirit, the latter rain, that will confirm everything that has been preached for the last 2000 years. We are right on the edge of this great outpouring. We are at the final hour! It is going to take a move of the Holy Ghost for God's plan to be fulfilled. But we have to be careful not to miss what God is doing.

Get Ready for Changes!

God never changes, but He emphasizes different things at different times in Church history. John the Baptist, for example, was sensitive to the fact that God was preparing him to point others to the next move of God — the ministry of Jesus. John said, "There's one coming who is mightier than I. I'm not worthy to unloose His shoes. I'm what God is doing now — I have the message of the hour, but don't stay here, because there is someone greater coming. I must decrease so He can increase."

He was trying to tell his followers that a change was coming, and when it came, they were to move with it. John 1:29 says, "The next day John seeth Jesus coming unto him, and saith, Behold the Lamb of God, which taketh away the sin of the world."

John's disciples watched while he baptized Jesus. He was saying, "Look, I've been talking to you about one coming who is greater than I. There He is!" But only two disciples left John the Baptist and followed Jesus. They weren't disloyal; they just saw the next wave coming. Before long, John's ministry was complete.

And later Jesus said, "I must go, because it's more profitable for you if I do" (John 16:7). The disciples didn't want Him to go, but His leaving led to the next move — the coming of the Holy Ghost, who would deliver to mankind everything Jesus purchased at redemption.

Two Groups of People

Today, we in the Church are standing at a fork in the road. The last teaching wave is waning, and a new wave is coming. People are running in two different directions. One group says, "I'm a Word person; don't give me all this Holy Ghost emotionalism!"

I thank God for the Word. It's the only thing that keeps us steady, renews our minds, gives us faith, and causes us to grow spiritually. Nothing replaces the Word.

Paul said in First Corinthians 2:

1 CORINTHIANS 2:1-5
1 And I, brethren, when I came to you, came not with excellency of speech or of wisdom, declaring unto you the testimony of God.
2 For I determined not to know any thing among you, save Jesus Christ, and him crucified.
3 And I was with you in weakness, and in fear, and in much trembling.

4 And my speech and my preaching was not with enticing words of man's wisdom, but in demonstration of the Spirit and of power:
5 That your faith should not stand in the wisdom of men, but in the power of God.

If we go with the Word only, people will have wonderful faith in man's wisdom and man's ability to proclaim the Word and bring revelation, but they won't have much faith in the power of God. If we get into trouble, we had better have faith in the power of God. The Word is first and foremost, but the Holy Spirit is the power that brings the Word to pass. We need a combination of the two.

Almost every move of God in the past 2000 years started out with *fire* and ended up with *ice* because they lost the move of the Spirit! They may have had some kind of Word message, but the minute they lost the move of the Spirit, they lost their fire. God had to find someone else to use.

The second group of people say, "We've found the move of the Spirit. We don't need the Word anymore. We don't need preaching or teaching." I've heard people say, "Church has been so great! We haven't had preaching for four weeks."

Sometimes God will emphasize certain themes over a period of time, but we shouldn't get excited because we don't have preaching or teaching. Teaching is our foundation. We will never leave the Word. God doesn't take away; He only adds to what has already been built.

So there are two extremes: We can either dry up and *blow* away because of too much Word and a lack of the Spirit, or we can *float* away. You may wish you could tie a spiritual rope around some people's ankles and reel them in out of the ozone. They walk around with a look that says, "I'm in the Spirit." They have forgotten to stick with the Word as their foundation.

We can go in one direction or the other. I don't know about you, but I would rather stand right in the middle of the road and hold on to both the Word *and* the Spirit.

Powerful Tools for Change

How is God going to accomplish His plan in these last days? He has been putting His Word out. And we're going to keep putting His Word out, preaching and teaching until Jesus comes. But we need the move of the Spirit of God.

When Jesus walked on the Earth, He had 12 disciples. In Luke 24:49, Jesus said, "...but tarry ye in the city of Jerusalem, until ye be endued with power from on high." Jesus ministered on this Earth for three and a half years. Up to this point, the disciples were able to ask Jesus anything they wanted. He answered their questions, met their needs, healed their bodies, took care of them, and fed them.

Most of us would think that if we had had three and a half years of being taught personally by Jesus, the job was complete; we were then ready to go and change the world!

Apparently when Jesus left, He knew these were the people He entrusted to go out and change the world. But after filling them with His Word, He said,

"It's still not enough. Don't move yet. You are not going to get the job done with the Word alone. Wait in Jerusalem until you are filled with power from on high. You will receive power after the Holy Ghost comes upon you."

He told them they had the Word, but they were not going to be witnesses for Him until they were endued with power from on high. We need a combination of both. We are not laying one aside for the other. God never takes what He has started, stops it, and picks up something else. No, He *adds* to it.

God is not taking anything away from what we call the "Word of Faith" or Teaching Revival; He is adding something to it.

The Mouth and Hand Connection

Let's look at the dedication of Solomon's Temple. King David wanted to build a house for God. But God said, "No, you've been a man of war, but your son will be a man of peace. I will have him build a house for Me."

In First Kings 8:15 at the dedication of Solomon's Temple, Solomon prayed, "You *spoke* it to my father David with your *mouth*, but you *fulfilled* it with your *hand*."

1 KINGS 8:15
15 And he said, Blessed be the Lord God of Israel, which SPAKE WITH HIS MOUTH unto David my father, and hath WITH HIS HAND FULFILLED it....

Now look at verses 23 and 24:

1 KINGS 8:23,24
**23 And he said, Lord God of Israel, there is no
God like thee, in heaven above, or on earth
beneath, who keepest covenant and mercy
with thy servants that walk before thee with
all their heart:
24 Who hast kept with thy servant David my
father that thou promisedst him: thou SPAKEST
also WITH THY MOUTH, and hast FULFILLED
IT WITH THINE HAND, as it is this day.**

How did God fulfill what He spoke to King David
about Solomon? How does He keep His covenant?
He *speaks* it with His *mouth* and *fulfills* it with His
hand. That's the way God accomplishes His will
and plan on this Earth. With His mouth He gives
us His Word.

But what is the "hand of the Lord"?

1 KINGS 18:46
**46 And the HAND OF THE LORD was on Elijah;
and he girded up his loins, and ran before Ahab
to the entrance of Jezreel.**

The hand of the Lord came on Elijah. The hand of
the Lord was the anointing, the power, the Spirit of
God. The Holy Ghost came on him.

"How's It Ever Going To Happen, God?"

Luke the first chapter tells us that an angel
appeared to a young maiden named Mary and talked
to her about the supernatural birth of the Lord Jesus
Christ. And she never doubted it. She was blessed
because she believed the Word. But she had one
question. The same one that floats through your

mind and my mind when we have seemingly impossible situations. She asked, "How shall this be...?" (Luke 1:34).

Many of us have the same question. We say to God, "The doctor said such-and-such, but You said I'm healed; how shall this be?" Or, "Lord, there are things You put in my heart about the future; there are things You showed me years ago. How shall this be?"

We've all done this, and we received the same answer Mary received in Luke 1:35: "...The Holy Ghost shall come upon thee, and the power of the Highest shall overshadow thee...."

The Word of God is what gives us faith and shows us what God will confirm. But the move of the Holy Ghost is what will bring it to pass. Many times we are doing everything right but nothing is happening. But God's plan always comes to pass the way it did in the Book of Genesis. Before God said, "Let there be light," the Spirit of God moved. The Word and the Spirit hooking up together bring the plan of God to pass.

A move of God, a revival, a mighty harvest, is coming. How shall this be? The Holy Ghost! God spoke it with His mouth, but He will fulfill it with His hand.

Years ago it was prophesied, "There will come a move or revival of the Holy Ghost and the gifts." We watched the Charismatic Movement come to pass. It was also said, "Then there will come a move of God which will be a revival of God and His Word." It was the Teaching Movement. And finally it was said, "Then there will come a move of God where the Word and the Spirit will come together; that will be

the greatest move of God the Earth has ever seen."
That is where we are now. We are on the edge of it.

For every move of God there are forerunners who
are brave enough to step out. They don't care what
anybody thinks about them. They are so hungry for
God, they will jump out and say, "All right, God,
here we are — we are available. We will take the
Word and the Spirit and run with the move of God."

In John 7:38, Jesus said, "...out of his belly shall
flow rivers of living water." Moving waters are a
picture of the move of the Holy Ghost. But people
are responding differently to this move. Some are
saying, "This river could rise and be dangerous. I'm
going to go to high ground and just watch."

But I believe God is thrilled with people who are
bold enough to say, "I sense that this is the Holy
Ghost moving. There is something about this
refreshing, cool water that I have to put my toes in it."

In Ezekiel 47, God took Ezekiel up in a vision
and showed him a river flowing out from the altar of
God to the Dead Sea.

EZEKIEL 47:3-5
**3 And when the man that had the line in his
hand went forth eastward, he measured a
thousand cubits, and he brought me through
the waters; the waters were to the ankles.
4 Again he measured a thousand, and brought
me through the waters; the waters were to the
knees. Again he measured a thousand, and
brought me through; the waters were to the
loins.
5 Afterward he measured a thousand; and it
was a river that I could not pass over: for the
waters were risen, waters to swim in, a river
that could not be passed over.**

God had an angel show Ezekiel the river, and he measured out a thousand cubits, or a third of a mile. The angel came back and got Ezekiel and walked him out in the river, and the waters were up to his ankles. Then he measured out another third of a mile, and the waters were up to his knees. He measured out another third of a mile, and the waters were up to his waist. Then he measured another thousand cubits. By this time, the waters were rising, and Ezekiel couldn't walk anymore. He just dove in and started to swim.

What's happening right now is the waters are starting to move from the altar of God toward the Dead Sea, or the world. God is walking us to the banks, measuring out a thousand cubits, and seeing if we will follow Him. If we do, He will take us out to ankle-deep water.

We will see people who will get out ankle deep, and they will enjoy it so much, they will stand there from now until Jesus comes, saying, "This water is wonderful! Let's stay here."

But God will have some people out of that group that He will walk out another thousand cubits to knee-deep water. And some will stay there the rest of their lives.

Then God will have another bunch who will go out waist deep. They will say, "This is wonderful; it couldn't get any better! Let's stay here."

There will even be people who will stand back on shore and won't put so much as their toes in the water, because they don't trust Him. They will say, "It's not what I expected."

If we will keep following on to know the Lord, we will go ankle deep, then waist deep, and then all of a sudden the waters will start to rise. When they do, the ones who have been standing on a safe place on the shore will find the waters too high to enter.

But if we follow Him, we will get so used to that water, we will dive in head first, it will wash us right into the sea, and we will be in the middle of the harvest.

God wants us to get our feet wet in the beginning of the move — to get refreshed with what He's doing now. He wants us to get in the river while it's moving slowly. It's a little shallow, and it's safe territory. Then when He sends the flood, it will wash us out into that swimming territory, and we will again be in the middle of what God is doing. When the spiritual dam finally breaks, and all the water comes flooding down, we will already be in the water. We will be washed downstream in the move of God while the others are still on high ground asking themselves, "I wonder if I ought to get in that move now?"

God wants us to step in the water, the moving of the Holy Ghost. We've had the Word, and now we are experiencing the move of the Spirit. The Word and Spirit are joined together, multiplying the power, the results, the flow — not just one or the other, but *both flowing together*.

Chapter 3

The Doorway to the Latter Rain

JAMES 5:7
7 Be patient therefore, brethren, unto the coming of the Lord. Behold, the husbandman waiteth for the precious fruit of the earth, and hath long patience for it, until he receive the early and latter rain.

James, writing to the Church, starts out by telling us to be patient.

What should we be patient for? *Unto the coming of the Lord!* During the last 2000 years, all kinds of theological discussions and doctrines about the Second Coming have floated through the Body of Christ.

However, in James' day, they didn't question whether Jesus was returning. They *knew* Jesus was coming back; in fact, they were ready for Him right then. That's why James' first point was: Jesus is coming back. That was important doctrine in the Church.

Every author in the New Testament said Jesus is coming back. The Lord Jesus Himself said, "Let not your heart be troubled: ye believe in God, believe also in me. In my Father's house are many mansions: if it were not so, I would have told you..." (John 14:1,2).

Jesus goes on to say, "And if I go and prepare a place for you, I will come again, and receive you unto myself; that where I am, there ye may be also" (John 14:3).

So Jesus said, "I'm leaving. I'm going to get a place ready for you, and when I get done, I'm going to come back for you." That's good news!

What Is God Waiting For?

So why hasn't Jesus returned already? James 5:7 says, "...the husbandman waiteth for the precious fruit of the earth...." Notice God calls Himself the "husbandman." You can find whole books that are based on the many names God has given Himself in the Word. Every name God has given Himself describes a part of His nature, character, ability, redemptive plan, and dealings with man so we can better understand Him. He is *Jehovah-Rapha*, *Jehovah-Jireh*, and *El Shaddai*, the God who is more than enough.

Then James calls God "the husbandman." Many translations call Him "the landman" or "the farmer." In the middle of all those wonderful, eloquent names, God calls Himself "the farmer," putting the term in light of the Second Coming. Why? Because there's something He wants us to understand.

James says, "Behold, the husbandman waiteth...." You don't have to know a great deal about farming to know that any good farmer takes time to prepare the soil, obtain the best seed available, plant that seed, and wait for the rain to fall. Everything the farmer does is geared toward one all-important moment in time — harvest.

No good farmer would ever work right up until harvest time and say, "I'm tired of this! I'm quitting and going home."

The Bible says that God the farmer is waiting for something. What is He waiting for? Is He waiting for Russia to attack Israel? No. Is He waiting for the signs of the times? No. They will be fulfilled just like He said. God is waiting for one thing: He is waiting for the harvest from His seed!

Earth's Best Seed

God "planted" the best seed this Earth has ever seen: His only begotten Son. Jesus Himself said, "...Except a corn of wheat fall into the ground and die, it abideth alone..." (John 12:24). Jesus called Himself a seed. As Peter said in First Peter 1:23, "Being born again, not of corruptible seed, but of incorruptible, by the Word of God, which liveth and abideth for ever."

We can see from this that Jesus is the seed. God planted that seed in the earth, raised Him from the dead, and elevated Him to sit at His own right hand, where He ever lives to make intercession for us. God is not going to allow the end of the age until He receives the harvest from His seed (Matthew 13).

It's hard to prepare for this harvest. We don't know what harvest looks like, because we've never seen one before. We simply have to follow the Holy Spirit and stay with God's Word.

Blueprint for Revival

However, God did give us a basic blueprint for revival when He gave us a picture of the planting season in the Book of Acts. Looking at the harvest from that standpoint, we see there were 120 people

present on the Day of Pentecost in the Upper Room.
That's not much of a start to reach the world with,
but it worked. They were all filled with the Holy
Ghost. Then they headed out to the streets and got
3000 saved the first day. Now there were 3120.

Several days later, Peter and John passed by the
crippled man at the Gate Beautiful and he was
healed. He leaped and praised God as he ran into
the synagogue. Peter followed him and preached
the Gospel.

The Bible says that 5000 men got saved that day.
That brings the total to 8120. And that is as if no one
went home and shared the Gospel with his family, in
which case that number could be multiplied by three
or four and added to the 8120 who were already
saved. And that wasn't even the harvest season;
that was still the planting season! If that is what
God did in the planting season, can you imagine the
mighty *harvest* He is preparing us for?

The Importance of the Rain

Notice James said the husbandman waits for the
precious fruit of the Earth until He receives *what*?
The early and the latter rain!

We in the Church world usually have our
attention focused on the return of Jesus. We should,
but notice what is going to take place before Jesus
comes back: *the harvest*. And what is going to bring
in the harvest? *The rain.*

So what we really ought to be doing is focusing
our attention on the rain, because once the rain
starts to fall, the harvest will come in, Jesus will
return, and we will go home.

But what *is* the rain? Hosea 6:3 says, "...he shall come to us as the rain, as the latter and former rain unto the earth." *The rain is simply a tremendous outpouring of the Holy Ghost upon the Earth.*

Thank God, through the blood of Jesus Christ, the door is open, and we can go into the presence of God any time we want. We can go boldly before the throne of grace to obtain mercy and find grace to help in time of need (Hebrews 4:16). But there are times when God brings His presence down to earth; times when He pours out His Spirit on this Earth. I like it when God visits us!

Visitations in the Church Age

There are two major visitations of God during the Church Age. One is called *the early rain*, and the other is called *the latter rain*. We have already seen the early rain in the Book of Acts, and we are just now stepping into the latter rain. We are stepping into what people have been expecting for 2000 years!

We are beginning to experience a few of the sprinkles right now. God is letting us know there is a Holy Ghost storm ahead of us like the one Elijah saw when he was praying and his servant reported there was a cloud on the horizon about the size of a man's hand. The prophet said, "Let's go! There's a storm coming!" That's what will bring the harvest in. That's what will produce and bring to fruition all the seed that has been planted for the past 2000 years.

Before we leave this world, there will be a greater manifestation of the glorious presence of God than we have ever seen before. This manifestation of God's presence — His glory — will be the greatest thing the world has ever seen.

As I studied the rain, the outpouring of the Holy Ghost, in the scriptures, I could see that Jesus is coming back, and the harvest is what will bring Him back. That's what He is waiting for. *But the rain is what will bring in the harvest.*

Spiritually Shipwrecked

There was a Latter Rain Movement in the '50s that caused some people to get off track. People can get so hungry for a move of God, they have a tendency to take anything that comes along and run off the deep end. Then they end up spiritually shipwrecked. In the past, sincere people could slip into some gray areas doctrinally and have time to get back in. Today we don't have time to drift off course and get back again.

If you left New York City heading for Los Angeles in a jet, you could be quite a bit off course by the time you reached Ohio, and still have time to adjust. By the time you reached Oklahoma, you would have less time to adjust. As you crossed the California line, you would have even less time. But by the time you reached Los Angeles International Airport, 40 feet off the runway, you had better be on target!

Spiritually speaking, this is where we are now. Five hundred years ago, 100 years ago, even 50 years ago, we had time to get sidetracked and then get back on course. But now we are about 40 feet from the runway, and we haven't time to get sidetracked with false doctrines and extreme teachings. We have to stay on course.

I began to pray about this. I said, "Lord, even the apostle Paul said, 'But I keep under my body, and bring it into subjection: lest that by any means, when I have preached to others, I myself should be a castaway' (1 Corinthians 9:27). If Paul had the potential to miss Your plan, even at the end of his ministry, then the rest of us surely have to be cautious. I want to stay steady and be able to finish my course."

I know the way to do this is: First, stick with the Word. Judge everything with the Word. Make sure it lines up with the Word. Second, follow the Holy Spirit, because He will always lead us back to the Word. The Spirit and the Word always agree.

I said, "Lord, if You have any other advice for me, I'd appreciate it." Soon after that, I began getting this phrase on the inside: "Rain is rain." I realized that rain never changes color or texture; the only thing that changes is the *amount* of rain that falls. Rain is always water, and it's always wet. If you've ever seen rain, you will always recognize rain. It always looks basically the same.

Planting rain is a slow, drizzling rain that prepares the soil for the planting of the seed. Harvest rain is a downpour that causes the seed to spring up for the harvest.

Comparing the Rains

I decided if I could find out what the early rain looked like, I'd know what the latter rain will look

like. Joel 2 talks about the rain, then describes it in
verse 23:

JOEL 2:23
23 Be glad then, ye children of Zion, and rejoice
in the Lord your God: for he hath given you the
former rain moderately, and he will cause to
come down for you the rain, the former rain,
and the latter rain in the first month.

Then in Acts 2:16,17, Peter stood up and said,
"But this is that which was spoken by the prophet
Joel...in the last days, saith God, I will pour out of
my Spirit...." This was the first pouring out or outpouring of the Holy Ghost in the Church Age, the
early rain. Notice God didn't say, "I will pour my
Spirit out." If He had, He has poured out everything
there is. Instead, He said, "I will pour *out of* my
Spirit." I like that. That means, "I've given you
some, but I've got a lot more left."

So Earth did not get all the Holy Ghost that
heaven has to offer on the Day of Pentecost. God has
reserved a lot more for the latter rain and for
outpourings in between.

You could say that the Book of Acts is the early
rain, and if you know what *early* rain looks like, you
will know what the *latter* rain looks like. Basically,
*the latter rain is going to look like the former rain
revisited on a worldwide scale.*

Recognizing the Genuine

When new moves come along, if we will just line
them up with the Word of God, we will be in safe

territory, and we won't have to wonder if they are strange or flaky. We won't have to get weird or become a reproach to the kingdom of God.

That's why I studied the Book of Acts. I got to the place where I thought I knew what the rain was going to look like. I thought I had it all settled in my mind: the blind will see, the lame will walk, the deaf will hear, and the dead will be raised in a mighty revival of healings and miracles — and we *will* see these things.

However, about the time you think you know something, something else will knock the props out from under you. Every door produces about 10 more on the other side, and the further you go, the more you see how little you really know.

But there was a truth in the Book of Acts I had skipped over; a part of the early rain I hadn't noticed. When the Day of Pentecost was fully come, Peter didn't have to explain to the devout Jews living in Jerusalem who Joel was. They knew what Joel had prophesied, and they were waiting for Joel's prophecy to come to pass. *But do you realize that when it started, they didn't recognize it?*

When the Holy Ghost fell, Peter had to stand up in the midst of these devout Jews and explain, "This is that which was spoken by the prophet Joel. *This* is what Joel talked about. It is what you have been waiting for and looking for, yet when it happened, you mocked and said, 'These men are full of new wine.'"

As someone said, "The amazing thing about the people who prayed the hardest and sought the most for a move of God back in the 1940s and 1950s was that they were the very ones who rejected it when it came." Why? *Because it didn't happen the way they thought it would!*

I found myself in the same spot. I had been waiting and praying for the rain for years. I had been studying about it. I knew exactly what it would look like, and I was watching for it. I was determined not to get sidetracked by anything else.

"What Do You Think?"

Then I held a meeting for a pastor friend — a man I've known for a long time — a man who knows the Holy Ghost as well as anyone I've ever met. There was another meeting going on across town, and I thought my friend would probably say politely, "I'm kind of staying away from it." I had heard it was quite strange.

Instead, he said, "Have you heard about the meeting across town?" He said, "I'll tell you one thing — it's God."

"It is?"

"Yes, it's God. I'm telling all my people to go over there every time we don't have a service and get a dose of it and bring it back here."

"Really?"

"Yes."

So he and I went to the other meeting the next day. The church was full of people. I'd heard that almost 8000 people had responded to the altar call in a six-week period, and they had baptized almost 4000 people. With results like that, I thought, *This must be the beginning of what I've been looking for. Maybe this is the beginning of the rain.*

I went expecting blind eyes to open, deaf ears to open, and the lame to walk. But after two hours, the only thing that was happening was what had been happening day and night for about six weeks. While the man was standing there preaching the Word, people were falling out of their chairs, drunk in the Holy Ghost, laughing.

I thought, *I wish they would quit that; I'm trying to hear him.*

Afterwards, my pastor friend asked me, "What do you think about it?"

I said, "Well, it's the Holy Ghost. The Holy Ghost isn't twins; that's for sure. There's no question about it."

"I know — but what do you think about it?"

"Well, it's the Holy Ghost. I don't have any problem with that."

"Yes, but what do you think?"

"It's Not My Style"

I said, "It's fine, but it's just not my style, okay? I'm waiting for the rain. I want the real thing. I haven't got time to get sidetracked."

A few months later, similar meetings were going on near our offices in Tulsa. One of our secretaries asked, "Have you heard about the meetings?"

"Yes, we've heard about them," I replied.

"Have you had a chance to go?"

"We just got in from overseas, and we've been kind of busy."

"Are you going to go?"

"I don't know. We went in another state."

"So you've been before?"

"Yeah."

"Well, what did you think?"

(I wished people would quit asking me this!) I said, "Well, it's the Holy Ghost."

"Yes, but what do you think?"

I said, "Well, it's just not my style, all right? Go and enjoy it if you like. I'm waiting for the rain. I want the real thing."

As I walked down the hall toward my office, I heard myself say, "That's not my style, and I pray to God He never uses me that way!"

As the old saying goes, "You'd better make your words sweet, because someday you may have to eat them."

The Glory of God Falls

Shortly after that, I was invited to speak at a campmeeting in another state. During one of the morning services as I was teaching, all of a sudden, in the middle of quoting a scripture, I heard myself say, "Aw, it's in there somewhere — you look it up!" I had never said anything like that in my life! I was getting scriptures twisted, and I couldn't even remember why I was using those scriptures, because I couldn't remember where my message was going!

Then I noticed my words were getting slurred, my tongue was getting all twisted — and I was having trouble walking straight! I wasn't doing this intentionally, mark my words. All of a sudden I thought, *Dear Lord, I'm drunk as a hoot owl!*

The Holy Ghost fell on me, even though I had said, "This is not my style." (God won't force anything on anyone, but I had also said, "God, I want to be in the middle of what You are doing," so I had thrown the door open.)

I couldn't walk right, talk right, or speak the verse that was the cap to my message. Finally I walked up to a man and said, "I can't get this verse out. Would you please read it?" He stood, took my Bible, and almost got through the verse. Then he started laughing and fell on the floor, drunk in the Holy Ghost.

I went to the next man. I said, "Would you please try to read this?" He stood up, started reading, got about halfway through the verse, started laughing, fell to the floor, and lay there laughing.

I went along the first two rows, and before long, everyone was lying on the floor under the power of God, drunk in the Spirit, and laughing. I thought, *Well, it's just this section. It's just these extremists.*

Then I noticed a certain sophisticated woman we have known for years sitting about four rows back. I thought, *She's not going to do anything strange.* I walked up to her and said, "Would you please read this for me?"

She took the Bible, looked at it — and all of a sudden hit the floor in the same condition as the rest!

God Ruins My Reputation

We never did get to my last verse. I was trying to say something, and the next thing I knew, I was flat on the floor, and in the distance I could hear the pastor trying to close the service. I was thinking, *God, You're going to ruin my reputation! I don't know what this is. I didn't ask for this. I don't even like this. It's not my style!*

That was Thursday morning. I had to wait until Saturday before I could go home, so I thought, *Well, I'm done. They have other speakers for the rest of the services. I'll just go and enjoy the meetings.*

On Thursday night, people went wild! As the power of God fell, the whole congregation took off dancing in the Holy Ghost and running the aisles. People were lying all over the floor.

As the power of God continued to fall, I felt myself sliding down in my chair. I thought, *I've got to get out of here! Maybe if I get some fresh air, I'll be all right.* I slipped out of the church to the speakers' room, where they had refreshments. I made myself a sandwich, poured a glass of iced tea, and began having dinner — all alone.

Soon I began feeling pretty much back to normal, and I realized I had been in the speakers' room for quite some time, but no one else had come. So I thought, *I'll go back and see what's happening. I don't want to miss anything.*

I looked into the auditorium through the windows in the big double doors. They were having church in there! As I stepped inside the auditorium through the double doors, a big, stocky usher we've known for a few years came walking toward me. He said, "Brother Mark, I've got to have more of this! Would you lay your hands on me?"

As I opened my mouth to say, "No, it's not on me. Go up and have someone in the front pray for you...,"

I felt my hand swat him right in the stomach! And when I did, he flew backwards and rolled under the stairway. At the same time, I flew backwards and lay on the floor wedged between the double doors. I couldn't get up. I finally rolled over and crawled into the hallway. I thought, *God, what are You doing to me? This is not my style. I don't even know if this is scriptural.*

Two Drunken Preachers

The next morning, the pastor came to my hotel to drive me to the airport. He brought a luggage cart up to my room on the fourth floor. We put my suitcases on the cart and got in the elevator. As we were heading downstairs, I looked at him and said, "In the Book of Acts when the Day of Pentecost was fully come, it says *suddenly* there came a sound. Have you ever noticed when the rain starts to fall, things happen suddenly?"

The minute I said that, the pastor flew back and hit one side of the elevator, and I flew back and hit the other side. By the time we got to the first floor, both of us were holding onto the luggage cart just to stand up. And we hadn't even checked out of the hotel yet!

When we got to the front desk, we could see the look of pity on the clerk's face. It was as if she were thinking, *Bless their hearts, it's not even noon yet. They claim to be preachers, and look at them — drunk!*

I got away from that meeting and thought, *I'm safe!* Then in January God spoke to Brother Kenneth E. Hagin about having Holy Ghost meetings, and he announced his first was going to be in Miami.

God dealt with us to change our schedule and go. We wanted so much to learn about the move of the Holy Ghost, and we thought, *Why not learn from someone who knows Him?* So we headed for Miami.

My Two Worst Fears Come True

As long as I've been a minister, two fears have dogged my trail. When I first started preaching, if I was to speak on a Sunday morning, I would wake up numerous times that Saturday night in a cold sweat. I had a recurring nightmare that I'd get up, stand in front of a crowd of people, and couldn't think of a thing to say. (Janet assures me this has never happened!)

The other fear I've had since I graduated from Rhema Bible Training Center was that one day Brother Hagin would be flowing in the Spirit, and he would look out over the congregation and say, "Brother Mark, I see you out there. Come up and share whatever God has given you."

I know people who have believed God to get *on* his platform, but I've always prayed to *stay off* the platform! I've had no desire whatsoever to get up there. Every time Brother Hagin would get "that look" on his face, I would slide down in my seat below everyone's head level or study the carpet intently.

So we got to the Holy Ghost meeting in Miami, and one night when the Spirit of God was moving, Brother Hagin said, "Brother Mark, I see you out there. Come up and share whatever God has given you." The minute he said that, I got a verse! I had something to share! God is so faithful!

Moving in Slow Motion

I got to the ministry area, and although I didn't see the glory cloud, it was like stepping into something, and I began moving in slow motion. As I climbed the steps to the platform, someone handed me the microphone, but I could not tell why I was there. I lost my verse somewhere about the third step. I had no idea what I was doing, so I just stood there.

Every time I tried to talk, I would break out laughing. I'd look at Brother Hagin for help, and he would double over laughing. He was no help at all! I'd look at the congregation for help, and they'd laugh. This kept going on and on for hours, it seemed, but it was probably for only three or four minutes. Then suddenly it was as if something blew across that platform, and I hit the floor again — wasted in the Holy Ghost. I lay there thinking, *There goes my reputation. God, this is not my style!*

You've got to understand I've been a teacher for years. I would know what direction to teach before the service even began.

I thought, *God, I don't understand this. I didn't ask for it. I don't even know if I like it or if it's scriptural! It's not my style. Besides that, I haven't got time for this. I'm waiting for the rain. I want the rain — the real thing!*

This Is That

Then I thought, *All right, if it's scriptural, it's in the Bible somewhere.* So I began to study the scriptures. I went back to the second chapter of Acts to look at the first outpouring of the Spirit of God on the Church. I read verses 15 and 16, where Peter said, "For these are not drunken, as ye suppose, seeing it is but the third hour of the day. But *this is that...*."

The Amplified Bible says, "This is [the *beginning* of] what was spoken through the prophet Joel." Peter didn't say that this is *all* of it; he said that this is the *beginning*. This is the doorway, the entrance, the first step into the rain. This is the preparation stage.

I thought, *All right, if Peter said this is the beginning of it, logic tells me if I go back a few verses, I'll probably see what the beginning of it was.*

I went back and read Acts 2:1-15 and found that 3000 were saved on the Day of Pentecost — but there were no blind eyes opened, no deaf ears opened, no lame walked, no lepers were cleansed, and no dead were raised. I could not find one physical healing miracle that occurred the whole day — but they got 3000 saved!

The only miracle I could find was that God took 120 people and got them so full of the Holy Ghost that when they went out of the Upper Room, they looked like they were drunk.

Rain Is Rain

I thought, *If rain is rain, probably the rain will begin at the end the same way it began at the beginning. The doorway to the rain is going to look the same.* And to get into the rain — to get to Acts 3, where the man at the Gate Beautiful was raised up — those early Christians first had to experience Acts 2.

Did you ever notice that there is this amazing progression in the Bible? To get to Acts 3, you have to go through Acts 2. It's a progression. We want all the blessings in the rest of the Book of Acts, but we must first experience Acts 1 and 2. In Acts 1, they prayed for an outpouring; in Acts 2, they stepped into it; and in Acts 3, they experienced the benefits of it. But first we must go through the door. Acts 2 is the door to the rest of the rain!

In other words, the rest of the Book of Acts is filled with signs, wonders, and miracles, but to get into the flow of the Holy Ghost, they had to get their tanks topped off with the Holy Ghost. To flow with the Spirit of God, they first had to get full of the Spirit of God. God wanted to reach the world, but He had to get the Church charged up first.

How could they step out and flow in *special faith* if they were too reserved to get full of the Holy Ghost and act a little strange? If they were too concerned about what people were going to think when they got drunk in the Holy Ghost, what would they do when God told them to go and pray for someone? They would still be thinking, *What will people say?*

Tired of Missing God

This applies to all of us. I've always been conservative, but I got so tired of missing God! I would finish a service, return to my hotel room, and repent to God for missing Him — not for doing something *wrong*, simply for not doing something *right*.

I got so tired of saying, "O God, I should have done this and that. The Holy Ghost was moving on me, and I should have done it, but, God, I'm kind of reserved, and when I sense the Spirit start to move, I think, *Maybe that's just me. What if I miss it?"*

Our "what ifs" keep us out of the blessings of God. God's Spirit rises up from inside us, but our minds reason it away, throw it out, and subsequently we miss God.

I decided I'd rather miss God by *doing it* than miss God by *not doing it* and cheating someone out of a blessing. I also found out that *when you get drunk in the Holy Ghost, you really don't care what other people think.*

I found out that *the way to get bold is to get full of the Holy Ghost.* When you get drunk in the Holy Ghost, you get bold (Acts 4:31). In the world, when people have a little too much to drink, they get bold. All they've got is a cheap substitute. We've got *the real thing* — the new wine!

Getting Bold

A while back, I was in a service and got loose in the Holy Ghost and was having a wonderful time. Without thinking, I heard myself say, "All right, there are two people here who have never danced in the Holy Ghost. You've always wanted to, but you are too timid. Just step out in the aisle and when I point at you, the Holy Ghost is going to come on you, and you're going to dance in the Holy Ghost."

Someone will ask, "What good will that do?" Jump in sometime, and you will find out. We are not talking about a learned two-step; we are talking about when the power of the Holy Ghost to dance gets in your feet. It takes you to a place in God that loosens a lot of other things in your life.

A man came walking across the front, and I thought, *What am I going to do now?* Without thinking, I pointed to him and said, "In the Name of Jesus!" He danced in circles across the front, rolled up against the platform, and lay there the rest of the evening.

Another fellow I'd known for years stepped into the aisle and just stood there. I said, "In the Name of Jesus!" — and when I pointed, his eyes got real big, his feet took off, and he danced down to the front, across the front, up the stairs to the balcony, all the way across the balcony, back down the stairs, and ran the next lap around the auditorium.

When he did that, the power of God radiated through the whole church, and the congregation went wild. The power of God saturated the whole place.

I looked at that and thought, *I could have done that a number of times through the years, but I held back. How many times have I missed God when someone really wanted something from Him and didn't get it because I didn't obey! Bless God, I'm going to stay loose in the Holy Ghost so I'll be bold enough to obey God.*

The First Sprinkles of the Latter Rain

These first sprinkles of latter rain are scriptural! This is the entrance, the beginning. If this sprinkling of rain is the beginning, think what the rest of the downpour will be like!

What is going on right now is not a man, a church, or a ministry. It's a move of God. And it's not limited to some ministries in some churches in some cities. It's what God is doing all over the world. It's the doorway into the latter rain, the last great harvest of the Church.

Chapter 4
Be Filled!

When the fire fell on the Day of Pentecost in Acts 2:1-4, God first filled the building. But that was not enough — He could do that under the Old Covenant (2 Chronicles 5).

Now there was a new and better covenant through Jesus' blood, so in the New Covenant, God could fill His new house, the Church, creating "living temples."

Acts 2:4 says, "And they were all filled with the Holy Ghost, and began to speak with other tongues, as the Spirit gave them utterance." *The first thing God did in the early rain was to fill the Church.*

God's continual instruction to the Church is found in Ephesians 5:17,18.

EPHESIANS 5:17,18
17 Wherefore be ye not unwise, but understanding what the will of the Lord is.
18 And be not drunk with wine, wherein is excess; but BE FILLED WITH THE SPIRIT.

"Be not unwise, but be filled with the Spirit" is a good, basic blueprint for God's will. The verb translated "be filled" in the Greek actually means "be *being* filled"; it is not just a one-time experience.

People say, "Well, bless God, I was filled back in 1923." It's one thing to *get* filled, but it's another thing to *stay* filled. I filled the gas tank when I bought our car, but I have to keep filling it.

The will of the Lord is to not be drunk with wine, but to be continually filled with the Holy Ghost. Luke wrote in Acts:

ACTS 2:1-4
1 And when the day of Pentecost was fully come, they were all with one accord in one place.
2 And suddenly there came a sound from heaven as of a rushing mighty wind, and it FILLED all the house where they were sitting.
3 And there appeared unto them cloven tongues like as of fire, and it sat upon each of them.
4 And they were all FILLED with the Holy Ghost, and began to speak with other tongues, as the Spirit gave them utterance.

Again, God filled the house first. God brought His presence down to the Church corporately. But it wasn't enough just to take His presence *to* the Church; He wanted to get it *in* the Church individually.

First God filled the *place*; then He filled the *people*. One hundred and twenty people were in the Upper Room, and they didn't stop and have a "Bless Me Club." There's something about getting filled that will push you out toward the lost, the sick, the depressed, and the needy. It puts fire in your bones and drives you to go find someone who needs God!

One hundred and twenty people is not much of a start for a Church that needs to reach the entire world, but it doesn't take many people if they are filled.

Jesus told His disciples to tarry in Jerusalem until they were endued with power. He knew what it would take to get the Gospel to the uttermost part of the

Earth — getting the people full of His power, His Spirit, Himself. So the first thing He did was fill people.

As we read, Acts 2 describes the early rain or the beginning of the Church. Since rain is rain, most likely the last or latter rain is going to start the same way the first rain started. If it took the infilling of the Holy Ghost to get the Church started, that's what it will take to get the Church to finish the job. If that's what it took to get the Church to plant the seed, that's what it will take to get the Church to harvest the seed.

The latter rain will begin in these days the same way the former rain began in Acts, when God took the existing Church, the 120, and filled them with His Spirit.

Running on Empty

When I was a kid, my mother drove a big Chrysler. She would run that car as dry as she could, and then buy $2 worth of gas. Then she would run it down and put another $2 worth of gas in it. My dad used to ask her, "Why don't you just run off the top of the tank and not the bottom?" It's not good for a car to let the gas tank get too low. When the tank gets low, all that junk in the bottom of the tank plugs the carburetor and can mess up the engine.

This is the same thing that happens to Christians. They run on fumes for a week, not taking the time to seek God in the Word or prayer. They take in all the junk from the world, and their lives are a mess. Then they roll into church Sunday morning, plop into a seat, and say, "Two dollars' worth, please!" If Christians would stay full, the world wouldn't be affecting them — they would be affecting the world!

People sometimes ask me to pray they would get a new job. They work with unbelievers who don't live right or talk right, and by the end of the day they are drained. We shouldn't let these things affect us. We should be so full of God and be such a strong influence at our work places that the unbelievers would say about us, "I don't know what it is about that person, but every time he comes in the room, I can't talk, act, or even think the way I usually do."

If we would keep our spiritual tanks full, we could influence the world instead of allowing the world to influence us. But the Church has been running on fumes. We need to get full of the Holy Ghost and *stay* full. We cannot get the job done when we are consumed with so many needs ourselves. We cannot be strong witnesses when our tanks are empty.

We want to see miracles, but revival has to start in us. God has to revive the Church before He sends revival to the world. I'm convinced through studying the Book of Acts that the first thing God wants to do is get us so filled with the Holy Ghost that we are filled to overflowing.

Even after three and a half years with His disciples, teaching and training them personally, Jesus wouldn't turn them loose to reach the world until they were endued with power or fire from on high. They had to be full before they could reach the world. Jesus put three and a half years' worth of fuel in them, but for that fuel to do its job, it had to come in contact with fire.

Saturating the Church

ACTS 2:1-4
1 And when the day of Pentecost was fully come, they were all with one accord in one place.
2 And suddenly there came a sound from heaven as of a rushing mighty wind, and it filled all the house where they were sitting.
3 And there appeared unto them cloven tongues like as of fire, and it sat upon each of them.
4 AND THEY WERE ALL FILLED....

Another meaning for "filled" is the word "imbue." I looked up this word and found it means "to be permeated or saturated." I thought, *That's what God is doing: He's saturating the Church!*

Using the word "saturate," we could read these two scriptures this way: "Be not drunk with wine, wherein is excess; but be *saturated* with the Spirit" (Ephesians 5:18). "And they were all *saturated* with the Holy Ghost, and began to speak with other tongues, as the Spirit gave them utterance" (Acts 2:4). *Filled* with the Spirit...*saturated* with the Spirit.

We need to treat ourselves like a dry sponge and not go to church to get *just enough* to get by until the next Sunday. We need to say, "God, I want to take everything I can get. I want to get so much in my life that if anyone gets within 10 feet of me, they're going to get wet!"

We'll be like Smith Wigglesworth riding on a train over in England. A man came to him, fell on his knees, and said, "My God, man — you convict me of my sins!" Wigglesworth hadn't said a word to him.

"Yes, but that was Wigglesworth."

No, it wasn't just Wigglesworth; *it was a man full of God.* If a man could get full of God back then, a man can get full of God today. And God is getting us good and full.

How To Get Saturated

People say, "How do you get saturated?" John 7:37,38, says, "In the last day, that great day of the feast, Jesus stood and cried, saying, If any man thirst, let him come unto me, and drink. He that believeth on me, as the scriptures hath said, out of his belly shall flow rivers of living water."

Notice Jesus didn't say, "If any man thirst, let him sit back and see what God might do." No, Jesus said, "...If any man thirst, let him come unto me and drink...." If we are thirsty, we must come to Jesus and do the drinking.

And what will be the result? Jesus said if we will come and start drinking, we will get so full that rivers will flow out of us! The drinking is for us; the rivers are for the world. But we are not going to have rivers for the world until we get full of what God is and what God has — until we are saturated with God Himself.

So how do we drink? I have heard people say, "If you are thirsty and want to get full of God, just keep drinking." I'd think, *Okay. But how do I do that? How do I drink?* I finally saw it the other day. I noticed when the Holy Ghost would begin to fall, every time people responded, whether it was shouting, jumping, dancing, or running, they were the first ones who appeared to be what we call "drunk in the Holy Ghost." I thought, *I've got it! I know how to drink: When the Holy Ghost moves, just move with Him.*

Every time we respond to the Holy Ghost, we take a drink of Him. Some people ask, "Why don't I ever feel anything?" Jump in and move with the Holy Ghost. Take a drink.

Others have thought, *If He makes me, I'll move.* That's like saying, "If He makes me get saved, I'll get saved." He won't *make* us do anything. But when the Holy Ghost starts moving, if we will jump in with Him, the Holy Ghost will hook us up with what is happening.

It doesn't matter if you run, dance, shout, or laugh — when the Holy Ghost starts moving, instead of having a backbone like a poker and saying, "I'm not going to do anything until God makes me," just jump in! I can say that because I'm as conservative as anybody in the world. I spent so many years saying, "I'm not going to do it if it isn't God. When God moves on me, I'll do it." I didn't want to be in the flesh.

Let me help you with that kind of thinking from firsthand experience. As long as we are on this Earth, we are going to be in the flesh. That's why Peter said on the Day of Pentecost, "For these men are not drunken, as ye suppose, seeing it is but the third hour of the day. But this is that which was spoken by the prophet Joel; And it shall come to pass in the last days, saith God, I will pour out of my Spirit upon all flesh..." (Acts 2:15-17). Notice Peter did not say God would pour out His Spirit on everybody's *spirit*. God said He would pour out His Spirit on all *flesh*. Some people spend their whole lives saying, "I'm waiting until I know it's God, because otherwise I might be in the flesh." Then they spend their whole lives *being in the flesh.*

Jesus didn't say, "If any man thirsts, let him sit back and see what happens"; Jesus said, "...If any man thirsts let him come unto me and drink...." "Him" in this verse has to do something. And what will be the result? That person will be filled or saturated with God.

Some people say, "I don't know about all this drunkenness." When the 120 in the Upper Room got filled or saturated with the Holy Ghost, there was an unusual response. Acts 2:12 says the religious leaders were in wonder, amazement, and doubt, saying, "What meaneth this?" In other words, when the 120 got saturated with the Holy Ghost on the inside, it showed up on the outside. Then Peter said, "These men are not drunken *as you suppose.*" He didn't say they weren't drunk; he said they weren't drunk on natural wine. They were drunk on the Holy Ghost wine!

I heard a minister say, "Life wasn't meant to go through sober." In life, things can get difficult. When things get tough for the unsaved, they head for the bar and get drunk to forget their problems for a few hours. But getting drunk only ruins their home, destroys their liver, and pickles their brain! The world has taken a cheap substitute and paid the price for it.

Paul said in Ephesians 5:18, "...be not drunk with wine, wherein is excess; but be filled with the Spirit...." There is no comparison between the world's excess wine and the Church's excess Holy Ghost.

What the world has makes them sick. What we have makes us healthy. What the world has takes their money. What we have prospers us. What the world has destroys their home. What we have puts ours together. What the world has gives them a hangover. What we have causes us to be full of joy!

The Church ought to know enough to get in the presence of God and get so saturated with the Spirit of God on the inside that it affects us on the outside.

Some say, "What about all this laughter? What's the purpose of it?" Psalm 126 says:

PSALM 126:1-3
1 When the Lord turned again the captivity of Zion, we were like them that dream.
2 Then was our mouth filled with laughter, and our tongue with singing: then said they among the heathen, The Lord hath done great things for them.
3 The Lord hath done great things for us; whereof we are glad.

If we believe our captivity has really been turned, we'll have laughter in our mouths. Jesus turned our captivity 2000 years ago.

In addition to that, the second Psalm says, "He who sits in the heavens laughs...." Someone will say, "That's fine for God. He's up there, and I'm down here with all my problems." No, Ephesians 2:6 says we've been raised up together with Him and made to sit in heavenly places in Christ Jesus. If we are seated with Christ where we are supposed to be, our problems will look much different. We'll be able to look at them from God's perspective, and we'll start laughing about them, too.

What about the dancing? In Second Samuel the sixth chapter, the Ark of the Covenant, which was the manifested presence of God on the Earth, had been absent from Jerusalem for about 20 years. When David became king, he immediately sent for the Ark of the Covenant to be returned to Jerusalem. David didn't want dead, dry religion; he knew the importance of having the manifested presence of God.

Second Samuel 6:14 says when David saw the Ark of the Covenant coming down the road, he danced before the Lord with all his might. He didn't dance simply because he was in a good mood; David danced because he came in contact with the presence of God.

Different people respond in different ways. Sometimes when we come in contact with the presence of God, it will get in our feet. Someone will ask, "What is that good for?" Have you ever tried to *explain* the New Birth to someone? You can teach, preach, or lead people into it, but you can't explain the New Birth. All I know is when I received Jesus, it changed my life. What about people dancing in the Holy Ghost? All I know is, it produces a freedom in the Holy Ghost never experienced before.

What about the running? In First Kings 18, we see there had been a drought for three and a half years, so Elijah began to pray for rain. He sent his servant out to look for the rain six times. Each time the servant said he could see nothing. Then, the seventh time, the servant said, "Well, there's a little cloud about the size of a man's hand." To the servant it was nothing, but to Elijah it was the beginning of the rain.

The Bible says the hand of the Lord came on Elijah when he saw that cloud, and he took off running 20 miles across the plains to the entrance of Jezreel, outrunning the king's chariot!

People ask, "Why do folks run?" Because they get a glimpse of something the rest of us haven't seen. The hand of the Lord comes on them, the Holy Ghost gets in their feet, and they get the same "run" on them that Elijah had.

It doesn't matter if we get drunk in the Holy Ghost, laugh, dance, or run. What God is doing is getting us so saturated that we respond somehow. We don't have to act like someone else or do what someone else is doing. We need to get full of God. If we lined up 15 people and had each one stick his finger into a light socket at the same time, each would get the same dose of electricity, but I guarantee every one of them would act differently. One thing for sure is that everyone would respond one way or another.

John G. Lake said, "Electricity is God's power in the natural, and the Holy Ghost is God's power in the supernatural." Often the Spirit of God will flow like electricity, and you know you can get saturated with electricity.

People say, "I don't understand why people act that way in church!" Have you ever come in contact with 110 volts? I have. I was getting ready for a service late one afternoon. I was in the Florida Panhandle where it gets hot and humid.

I had flown in earlier that day, had picked up a rental car, and had driven to the hotel. I went in to take a quick shower before church, and the steam must have set off the smoke alarm in the hotel room. It was blaring.

I thought, *I've got to get this thing turned off so I can get ready for church!* I didn't want to wait for a maintenance man; I wanted to turn that alarm off *now*.

I knew some smoke alarms operated on 9-volt batteries and assumed this one did also, so I thought I'd take the alarm off the wall, remove the battery, and everything would be fine.

Saturated With Electricity

When I reached up and pulled the alarm off the wall, I quickly found out it was not one of those alarms that operated on a 9-volt battery, but rather on a 110-volt electrical system. The wires came undone, my arm touched them, and remember, I was standing in a puddle of water, having come out of the shower. When you come in contact with electricity, you'll respond.

People say, "I don't understand people running, shouting, laughing, and crying." I did all of that at the same time! I ran around the room, jumped, danced, shouted, yelled, laughed, and cried. My body buzzed for about two hours.

I had a brush with electricity, and I got *saturated* with it. If you can get saturated with electricity, you can get saturated with the Spirit of God.

Someone will say, "That's fine, but give me chapter and verse." I was hoping you'd ask. I don't expect people to accept anything unless it can be proved from the Bible.

The Tangible Anointing

Look at Acts 19:11,12:

ACTS 19:11,12
11 And God wrought special miracles by the hands of Paul:
12 So that from his body were brought unto the sick handkerchiefs or aprons, and the diseases departed from them, and the evil spirits went out of them.

In other words, Paul was praying for the sick with *a tangible anointing*. The Spirit of God was flowing through his hands. However, there were sick, bound, and oppressed people who couldn't get to where Paul was with that anointing.

So God apparently gave Paul a revelation that the anointing could saturate pieces of cloths as he laid hands on them. Then friends and relatives would take the cloths to the sick, and the sick people would get healed. Why? Those cloths would operate like a storage battery. The anointing would be stored in the cloths and then go into the bodies of the sick when laid upon them.

If God can saturate a piece of cloth to the point that it can set the captives free, don't you think He can saturate a New Testament believer? If that anointing can flow into a piece of cloth, why can't it flow in and saturate us?

One Baptism, Many Refillings

People say, "Either you have the Holy Ghost or you don't." No, there is always room for more. There is one *baptism*, but there are many *refillings*. We get a *measure* of the Spirit when we are born again. When we are baptized in the Holy Ghost, there is more yet. Then all through life, there should be constant refillings of the Holy Ghost. We see this throughout the scriptures. Jesus Himself said in His earthly ministry in Matthew 5:6, "Blessed are they which do hunger and thirst after righteousness, for they shall be filled" — or saturated.

Paul prayed in Ephesians 3:19, "that you might be filled with all the fullness of God." What is the fullness of God? That means filled with God Himself. What is God filled with? He's filled with His Word, His Spirit, His life, His wisdom, and His understanding. If Paul prayed this for the Christians in Ephesus, how much more should we be praying this prayer?

The Double Portion

Another scriptural example of saturation is found in Second Kings 2, the story of the prophet Elijah and his successor Elisha. Elisha followed Elijah and operated in the helps ministry for about 15 years.

Elijah knew his time on Earth was nearly over, so he said to Elisha, "You've been faithful. What do you want?" Elisha replied, " I want a double portion of the anointing of God that is on your life."

Elijah said, "You've asked a hard thing, but if you see me when I go, you'll get it."

Of course, Elisha kept his eyes on Elijah until the time when he was caught up in that whirlwind. And as he was caught up, the mantle he was wearing fell from heaven. Elisha picked it up, tore up his own mantle, and stepped into the fullness of his calling.

One Miracle Short

If you follow his life, you will find that Elisha worked exactly *twice* as many miracles as Elijah did — except when he died, he was one miracle short.

Every spring, the Moabites sent teams to attack the Israelites. One of the Israelites had died, and his friends were about to bury him, but they saw a team of Moabites coming after them. They had to get rid of the body in a hurry, so they dropped it into the nearest tomb. They didn't notice it was Elisha's tomb.

When the man's body landed on the bottom of the tomb, it landed on a set of bones — *Elisha's* bones. Second Kings 13:21 says that when that body landed on those bones, the man revived or was raised from the dead!

I'm sure it shocked him when he came back to life and realized where he was. He probably leaped out of that tomb in one bound and took off running after his friends.

The bottom line is this: If God in the Old Testament could saturate a man so much that even after he died there was enough anointing left in his *bones* to raise someone from the dead, don't you think He could saturate the life of a believer in the New Testament?

God Manifested on the Earth

We must understand the tangibility of the Spirit of God. He is the Third Person of the Trinity: Father,

Son, and Holy Ghost. *He is God manifested on this Earth today.* And He will saturate us.

The Holy Ghost is a real Person. He will move in us when we are born again. He will saturate us when we are baptized in the Holy Ghost. We can get more and more saturated throughout our lifetime.

We are coming up to the greatest hour the Church has ever seen, called *harvest*, when we will reach out and bring in multitudes of lost people. We must have great strength and power to get this job done. We will get this strength and power from a combination of the Word and the Spirit of God saturating us.

God is saturating us for this task. That is why we are having services where we get filled with the presence of God — not to have an outward feeling or experience but to experience an inward change.

The Easy Way To Change

Someone will ask, "Why should we get full of God?" Because that's the easiest way to get changed.

"But I don't need to be changed." Check again.

Someone else will say, "Oh, brother, I've been trying to change for years." Give up. If something doesn't work, you need to do something different. You can't produce change on your own.

Most of the habits, problems, and difficulties we want to change were supernaturally caused to start with, and it's going to take something supernatural to get them off us. It doesn't work to fight supernatural bondage with natural strength. Those things do not get off our lives by our own might or power, but by the Spirit of God.

If we keep feeding on the Word, building up our inner man, and allowing the Holy Ghost to manifest Himself, we will turn into "Teflon Christians." Nothing the devil offers will be able to stick to us! Whether it's spirit, soul, or body, there is something about getting into the presence of God that will change us more quickly than anything else in the world.

Changed by the Glory

The Lord Jesus Christ Himself when He walked on this Earth took three of His disciples — Peter, James, and John — up on the Mount of Transfiguration, and the glory came down. His disciples saw Jesus talking with Moses and Elijah in the glory! They noticed His garments were white and glistening, and His face began to shine. He was transfigured or changed.

If the glory will change Jesus — who didn't need any changing — think of what His power and presence will do for us!

Changed Into the Same Image

Paul, writing under the inspiration of the Holy Ghost, said in Second Corinthians 3:18:

2 CORINTHIANS 3:18
18 But we all, with open face beholding as in a glass the glory of the Lord, are CHANGED into the same image FROM GLORY TO GLORY, even as by the Spirit of the Lord.

To give you a quick background, this scripture is referring to Moses. Moses had a congregation of

3 million people, none of whom was born again, since the New Birth wasn't available yet. Because of this, the children of Israel had problems staying out of trouble. At one point, Moses went up on Mount Sinai and spent 40 days in the manifested presence of God.

While Moses was up in the glory, God took two tablets of stone, moved His finger, and wrote a 10-point message on them. Moses had a sermon! In fact, he had enough messages to preach for the next 10 weeks or maybe more. He had the message to curb sin in the camp. He had heard from heaven. He had what he had been looking for. He had a wonderful time during those 40 days in the presence of God.

As he was coming back down the mountain, he heard music and dancing. But as he got a little closer, the music didn't sound quite right. As he got closer still, he realized not only was the music not right, but all 3 million Israelites were worshiping a cow — the golden calf!

The High Priest's Excuse

Moses walked up to his brother Aaron and asked, "What happened here?"

Aaron said, "I don't know, man. We had a fire going under that big pot over there, and people kept walking by and throwing in their gold earrings. The next thing I knew, this gold cow jumped out. We figured it was supernatural, and we probably ought to worship it." Aaron knew he was in trouble!

Moses lost his sanctification. He had been up in the glory for 40 days, and when he came back, he found the whole camp worshiping a golden cow! He got mad and threw the tablets down, thus losing his 10-point message. Moses ground up the golden calf, spread the gold on the water, and made the people drink it!

A Preacher's Lament

In Exodus 33:18, we find Moses saying, "I beseech thee, shew me thy glory." In other words, "I spent 40 glorious days with You and had to come back and deal with church problems — *now* what am I going to do?" God said, "Come up again."

Often we get in the presence of God and think, *Once or twice is enough.* However, I want to get in every meeting I can possibly get into — teaching, preaching — whatever it is. I want to get in the presence of God every time I can.

Once wasn't enough for Moses. He had a message to help the people, but it still wasn't enough. God called him up again, for 40 more days. That's 80 days total — almost three months of being in the manifested presence of God.

The first 40 days produced temporary help. But when Moses came down the second time, the people saw he was saturated with God to the extent his face was glowing like a human light bulb.

The people said, "Put a veil over your face, Moses. We can't stand to look at you." The first trip into the glory of God gave him a message; the second 40 days changed him.

That is what Paul was referring to in Second Corinthians 3:18 (*Amp.*), when he said, "But we all, with open face [or with our veils lifted] beholding [or looking] as in a glass [a mirror] the glory of God...."

When you look into a mirror, who do you see? You see yourself. If you happen to look into a mirror and see the glory of God, who is it on? You. So the subject Paul is still talking about is getting the manifested presence of God in and on our lives.

Notice Paul said we are changed *from glory to glory*. It's not getting in the glory one time; it's getting in from glory to glory to glory until we are so *saturated on the inside* that it shows up on the outside.

When we get full of God, saturated with His presence, changes are going to take place. On the Day of Pentecost, 120 intimidated believers got saturated with the presence of God and were transformed into flames of fire to change their world.

What is God doing today? He is getting us so full of Himself that there is nothing that can hold us back. We are being saturated with the Holy Ghost so we can be containers — earthen vessels filled with the excellency of His power!

Chapter 5
Days of Joy and Refreshing

Many wonder about the unusual moving of the Spirit of God that we are seeing in the Church today. It's what Peter calls "joy unspeakable" in First Peter 1:8 — so much joy on the inside that it can't be spoken out, so it often manifests in a laugh, a shout, a dance, or even a run. It is God restoring joy to the Church.

Some have said, "But I thought we were supposed to be quiet and *reserved* in church." Religious thinking has said for years that it is *spiritual* to cry in church but *carnal* to laugh in church. Where do you suppose that thought originated? The Bible refers to rejoicing far more than it does weeping. There is a time to weep, but there is also a time to rejoice.

The Church has been in the ditch for years concerning weeping. We've thought that to experience the glory of God, we have to be somber. But Psalm 149:5 says, "Let the saints be joyful in glory...." Getting into the presence of God will fill us with joy like we've never known before. That's why David the psalmist could say in Psalm 16:11, "...in thy presence is fulness of joy...." He had experienced firsthand the joy that comes from the presence of God.

Joy on the Inside

Joy not only comes from being in the presence of God, but joy is deposited on the inside of believers when they are born again. Romans 14:17 says, "For the kingdom of God is not meat and drink; but

righteousness, and peace, and joy in the Holy Ghost."
Righteousness, peace, and joy in the Holy Ghost are
three things God has put inside us. The minute we
are born again, we are made righteous. "For he hath
made him to be sin for us, who knew no sin; that we
might be made the righteousness of God in him" (2
Corinthians 5:21).

Peace and joy are both fruits of the spirit which
are deposited inside us at the New Birth (Galatians
5:22), so these ought to be signs of the believer. Most
people expect joy to start outside and work its way
inside; however, God starts on the *inside* and works
things to the *outside*.

Just Laugh at the Circumstances!

The world can experience some happiness, but
their happiness is determined by situations. People
are happy one day and unhappy the next. Their
emotions go up and down like a yo-yo. One minute
they will say, "Everything is going great. I'm on top
of the world today!" The next minute they will say,
with their chin dragging the ground, "My life is
falling apart."

On the other hand, joy is not affected by situations
or circumstances. It has nothing to do with what's
happening on the outside. Joy has to do with what
has been deposited on the inside.

If we would stop allowing the things on the
outside to affect our lives, and reach down on the
inside and start rejoicing, the direction of our lives
would be changed.

We may not always feel like rejoicing. Someone once said to Smith Wigglesworth, "You never change. I know you have trouble like everyone else, but you are always the same; you are always on top of everything. How do you do it?"

Wigglesworth replied, "When I get up in the morning, I never *ask* Smith Wigglesworth how he is. I take him to the Bible and *show* him how he is."

We often get up and say, "I feel down today, and I know everything is going to go wrong." What we ought to be doing is seeing what the Word says about us and then having a good laugh at all the problems. We ought to experience the joy that has been deposited on the inside of us.

Finding the Joy Within

Remember what it was like when you were first saved? For a few hours, days, or weeks, nothing mattered. You didn't care what anyone thought, what your body felt like, or what was in your bank account. All of a sudden you passed from death to life, and you were going to heaven. There was so much joy in your life, you didn't care what happened. Nothing made any difference. Your car could have stopped running, or you could have lost your job, but you had so much joy, nothing else mattered. It was just so good to be free!

Then people started giving you "reality pills," saying, "In a little while you will come down with the rest of us." All of a sudden, that joy was gone. But joy is a fruit of the human recreated spirit. Fruit shouldn't decrease; it should increase.

They Need What We Have!

Yet the psalmist David asked God to restore the joy of his salvation. I believe that is what God is doing in the Church today.

> **PSALM 51:12,13**
> **12 RESTORE UNTO ME THE JOY of thy salvation; and uphold me with thy free spirit.**
> **13 Then will I teach transgressors thy ways; and sinners shall be converted unto thee.**

The psalmist is saying, "If you can restore the joy I had when I started, I'll start getting sinners converted to you."

One of the reasons we haven't been reaching the lost is because we haven't had much with which to reach them. For years, the lost have looked at the Church and said, "Dear God, I don't want what they have; it could be contagious." The Church needs to get back to where the world looks at us and says, "They have something I don't have, and I want it!"

When we start getting back to that place of joy, we will see people restored and sinners converted. But joy has to be restored to the Church first.

When Joy Is Lost

As noted before, many Old Testament scriptures have a twofold meaning, initially foretelling events that would take place in their day as well as looking into the future and describing events that would take place in the last days. Joel 1:11,12, for example, could easily point in both directions.

Let's look at this passage of scripture in the light of where we are today.

JOEL 1:11,12
11 Be ye ashamed, O ye husbandmen; howl, O ye vinedressers, for the wheat and for the barley; because the harvest of the field is perished.
12 The vine is dried up, and the fig tree languisheth; the pomegranate tree, the palm tree also, and the apple tree, even all the trees of the field, are withered: because JOY IS WITHERED AWAY from the sons of men.

In verse 11, the Holy Ghost through the prophet Joel describes a sad situation pertaining to husbandmen or farmers. The vine, the fig tree, and all the other fruit-bearing trees of the field are not producing fruit. The end of verse 12 says this is because the sons of men have lost their joy!

Often in the scriptures, the fig tree is a type of Israel, and the vine is a picture of the Church. All the other trees could be giving us a look at the nations or Gentiles. If all three groups are barren because joy has been lost, it could be said that if joy were restored to the Church, it would affect the other groups. This is what happened on the Day of Pentecost.

When the existing Church of 120 people got full of the Holy Ghost and joy, it immediately began to touch the Jews in Jerusalem. Then it spread to other Jews and to Gentiles, as is recorded throughout the Book of Acts. But this did not happen until Holy Ghost joy was deposited inside each one.

When Joy Is Restored

The devil has deceived the Church into thinking that the world says we are crazy if we act like we are free. We have been in churches all over the country where they want to stifle the moving of the Holy Ghost in their services. They say, "Let's stay calm and sophisticated. What would we do if the mayor showed up?" The mayor wouldn't show up if he wasn't looking for something better than what he already had.

I've never seen the Holy Ghost offend anyone. Over the past few years, I've seen more sinners born again and more backsliders get right with God in these Holy Ghost meetings than I've seen in many evangelistic meetings. There's something about the world coming in and seeing the Church enjoying our relationship with God that gets their attention. Notice what happens in Psalm 126:

> **PSALM 126:1-3**
> **1 When the Lord turned again the captivity of Zion, we were like them that dream.**
> **2 Then was our mouth filled with laughter, and our tongue with singing: then said they among the heathen, The Lord hath done great things for them.**
> **3 The Lord hath done great things for us; whereof we are glad.**

Then said they among the heathen, "That bunch down there is crazy. I wouldn't hang around them for anything in the world." Did they say that? No. "...Then said they among the heathen, The Lord hath done great things for them."

When the Church gets filled with the Holy Ghost and joy, the world is going to look at us and say, "God is doing something for them." Being strictly religious for 2000 years hasn't gotten the Church anywhere.

We might as well do something different. It's about time we got full of joy.

The Church is about to experience the greatest move of God anyone has ever seen. This last great move is beginning the same way the first great outpouring did — with an outpouring of joy. When joy is restored to the Church, it will not only change the Church; it will touch the world.

On the Day of Pentecost, 120 believers had their lives changed. Then almost immediately 3000 people were born again. Those early Christians who attracted the world in that day were speaking with tongues and had such joy, the world thought they'd had too much to drink. *Joy still gets the attention of the world.*

Joy That Transforms

We have a Bible school to train ministers in Tallinn, Estonia. The people of Estonia had been under communist rule for 40 years prior to 1991. Communism frowned on any form of emotion, saying it was a sign of weakness. As a result, these people were very hungry for God, yet very unemotional.

Suddenly joy began to explode in the classroom! There was laughter, dancing, and running. This was nothing they had ever seen before — it was an outpouring of the Holy Ghost. The lives of the students were dramatically changed. Many were changed from timid to bold. They began getting people born again on the streetcars when asked why there was such joy on their faces.

Another example of the effects of this outpouring of joy is a woman who shared with us how she had lost a loved one a few months earlier. She was so overcome with grief that she was planning to take her own life the next week.

She explained to us that the previous night she became "drunk in the Holy Ghost" in the service and was flooded with joy. When she finally went home that night, she noticed that even though she missed her loved one, the grief was gone, and she no longer wanted to die, but live. The joy of the Lord has become her strength (Nehemiah 8:10).

The Never-Ending Well...

We in the Church world have lived far below our rights and privileges. Defeat, discouragement, and depression are not part of God's plan for the Church.

> **ISAIAH 12:3**
> **3 Therefore with JOY shall ye draw water out of the wells of salvation.**

Isaiah says that we draw water out of the wells of salvation *with joy*. The minute we are born again, wells of salvation are deposited on the inside of us. One Bible dictionary describes salvation in this way: "Salvation is the sum total of all the blessings bestowed on man, by God, in Christ, through the Holy Spirit." Salvation is a package deal. It includes everything: deliverance, divine protection, healing, health, prosperity, wisdom — the life, nature, and ability of God.

Some people are unable to receive the blessings of salvation because their "bucket" is broken. Their bucket is full of holes and can't draw anything out of the well. We have a well full of the blessings of salvation — a well full of healing, a well full of prosperity, a well full of deliverance — but every time the bucket goes down in the well, it comes up empty. Why? With *joy* we draw water out of the wells of salvation. We will never get the full benefits of salvation until our joy is restored.

So God is restoring joy to the Church today — not so we can have a "Bless Me Club," but to send us to the world.

Drawn to the Harvest

On the Day of Pentecost, God filled 120 people with the Holy Ghost; they were wall-to-wall Holy Ghost. But did you notice, it didn't just benefit them? They were so full of the joy of the Holy Ghost, it drove them into the harvest fields.

The Holy Ghost fell in the morning, and by 9 o'clock they were on the streets reaching the lost. There is something about getting full of God that will drive you to the masses.

Why is God restoring joy to the Church? Because there is a world to harvest and joy is part of our supernatural equipment to do the work. *The only Bible most of the world is ever going to read is us.* Second Corinthians 3:2 says, "Ye are our epistle written in our hearts, known and read of all men...." The only Church the world is going to come in contact with is what we take to them, so we must have something they don't already have. The devil has cheap substitutes for many things, but one thing he cannot substitute is joy. When the world sees joy in the Church, it will get their attention!

The Scriptural Basis

A minister friend told me, "I have been going all over the country preaching about the return of Jesus, the harvest, and the rain. I have been telling people we ought to be fervently praying, weeping, and groaning. But when I preach this, people start laughing, dancing, running, and getting drunk in the Holy Ghost! We are not seeing the weeping and wailing. We are seeing people refreshed and recharged. I don't understand it. What is happening?"

I shared how I had experienced the same things and had the same questions. God's Word, however, has all the answers. I knew if this was a move of God, it would have to be referred to numerous times throughout the Word, so I began to search the scriptures. Not only did I find a scriptural basis for what was happening in services, but I would have been surprised if it was *not* happening.

Signs of the Times

What is the scriptural basis for this seemingly unusual outpouring of the Holy Ghost? Paul said in First Thessalonians 5:1, "But of the *times and the seasons*, brethren, ye have no need that I write unto you." We can gain more insight into this statement by what Jesus said in Matthew 13 when He upbraided the Pharisees for not being able to read the *signs of the times*.

Anytime God is about to do something major on the Earth, He will produce signs to prepare people for that event. First Chronicles 12:32 says, "And of the children of Issachar, which were men that had *understanding of the times*, to know what Israel ought to do...." All through the scriptures, God described signs that would occur prior to the return of Jesus. Is the refreshing move of God we are experiencing now a sign of the times?

In Acts 3:19, Peter said, "Repent ye therefore, and be converted, that your sins may be blotted out, when the times of refreshing shall come from the presence of the Lord...." Notice Peter said *times* — not just one time, but times, plural.

The local church can't exist on wild Holy Ghost services only. We need preaching and teaching — not a wild Holy Ghost hoedown every service. We can't be running the aisles, jumping the pews, and swinging from the chandelier every service. In the Church we must have the whole counsel of God, yet God told us in the scriptures there would be times of refreshing.

Times of Refreshing

Peter said these times of refreshing would come from the presence of the Lord. The next verses say, "And he shall send Jesus Christ...whom the heaven must receive until the times of restitution of all things..." (Acts 3:20,21).

Peter joins together times of refreshing and the return of Jesus! When Peter says, "And he shall send Jesus...," he can't be talking about the first coming of Jesus, because He had already come the first time.

Peter must be referring to the return of Jesus for the catching away of the Church. So apparently what Peter is saying is that before Jesus returns, there will come a great refreshing to the Church.

This outpouring of rejoicing, refreshing, laughter, joy, and drunkenness in the Holy Ghost is not some side issue, but a sign of the times. If it were only taking place in one city, it wouldn't mean a great deal, but when this goes from nation to nation and continent to continent on a worldwide scale, it is not just a move; it is an outpouring of the Holy Ghost and a sign of the times. What are the times? Times of refreshing, and He shall send Jesus. They are joined back-to-back.

Someone will say, "Yes, but I want at least two verses for that." Good, I was hoping you would ask. Someone once said that the key to Bible interpretation is to find out who is doing the talking, who is being talked to, and what is being talked about. In Second Peter 1:1, the apostle Peter is writing to "them that have obtained like precious faith," or the believers.

The Last Days

2 PETER 3:1-4,10
1 This second epistle, beloved, I now write unto you; in both which I stir up your pure minds by way of remembrance:
2 That ye may be mindful of the words which were spoken before by the holy prophets, and of the commandment of us the apostles of the Lord and Saviour:
3 Knowing this first, that there shall come in the last days scoffers, walking after their own lusts,

**4 And saying, Where is the promise of his com-
ing? for since the fathers fell asleep, all things
continue as they were from the beginning of
the creation.**
**10 But the day of the Lord will come as a thief
in the night; in the which the heavens shall
pass away with a great noise, and the elements
shall melt with fervent heat, the earth also and
the works that are therein shall be burned up.**

So Peter is talking to the Church, and he is
talking about the return of Jesus.

The Promise of Jesus' Return

GALATIANS 2:7,8
**7 But contrariwise, when they saw that the
gospel of the uncircumcision was committed
unto me, as the gospel of the circumcision was
unto Peter;**
**8 (For he that wrought effectually in Peter to
the apostleship of the circumcision, the same
was mighty in me toward the Gentiles.)**

Even though Peter was writing to the Church,
his ministry was specifically directed to the Jews
(circumcision). With Peter's primary calling being to
the Jews, he would say things that were more
familiar to the Jewish mind or background. His
writings would relate to those with a greater
knowledge of Old Testament scriptures. With that in
mind, let's look at Second Peter 3:8.

2 PETER 3:8
**8 But, beloved, be not ignorant of this one
thing, that one day is with the Lord as a**

thousand years, and a thousand years as one day.

While Peter is talking about the return of Jesus, he adds, "With the Lord one day is as a thousand years, and a thousand years as a day." Remember, Peter is talking to the Jewish mind, knowing this should cause them to refer back to the Old Testament; specifically, Hosea 6:2,3.

> **HOSEA 6:2,3**
> **2 After two days will he revive us: IN THE THIRD DAY he will raise us up, and we shall live in his sight.**
> **3 Then shall we know, if we follow on to know the Lord: his going forth is prepared as the morning; and he shall come unto us as the rain, as the latter and former rain unto the earth.**

The Great Reviving

The prophet Hosea is talking about the *latter* rain; therefore, this scripture is also referring to New Testament times. Notice what Hosea said in reference to the rain: "After two days will he revive us: in the third day he will raise us up, and we shall live in his sight" (Hosea 6:2). Being raised up and living in His sight sounds like the catching away of the Church.

Look closely at what Hosea said: "After **two days** he will *revive* us: in the **third day** he will *raise us up*, and we shall *live in his sight*." Peter said, "...one day is with the Lord as a thousand years...." So after two days or 2000 years we should expect a great reviving.

We have often thought that verse referred to revival in the world, but the world can't experience revival. You can't revive something that is dead! "Revive" means to bring back or restore to life. *Revival is for the Church.*

The Church in Time

Hosea said, "After two days, or 2000 years, He will revive us." Where is the Church in reference to time? This move of God we are seeing in the Church world today began to gain momentum on a worldwide scale about 1995. History tells us that Jesus was born about 5 B.C. If we add those years together, it brings us to approximately 2000 years since His first coming.

So we should expect at the end of a 2000-year period to have a great reviving come to the Church. And this is where the Church is right now! We are approximately 2000 years from the first coming of Jesus.

Look again at what Hosea said. "After two days or 2000 years He will revive us, and in the third day or third thousand years He will"— what? "Raise us up, and we will live in His sight." Did you notice what Hosea said would come back-to-back? After two days or 2000 years, there will be a great reviving, and as we move somewhere into that third day or third thousand-year period, He is going to raise us up, and we are going to live in His sight. We don't know *when* He'll raise us up in that third day, but we do know that when God raised Jesus from

the dead, He raised Him *very early* on the third day
(Luke 24:1-3).

I would be shocked if we weren't seeing a
rejoicing, joyful, reviving time in God. Revival doesn't
mean we are on our faces crying and weeping.
Revival means He is restoring us back to life. He is
restoring the joy we lost through the ages.

Bringing in the Sheaves With Joy

Let's look at one more passage of scripture that
verifies that the current move of the Holy Ghost is a
sign of the times. Psalm 126:6 says, "He that goeth
forth and weepeth, bearing precious seed, shall
doubtless come again with rejoicing, bringing his
sheaves with him."

For 1900 years, the Church has been going forth
weeping, bearing precious seed. That precious seed is
the Word of God. The work of the ministry has been
plowing new territory and planting seed — taking
the Gospel to countries where people haven't heard.

Psalm 126:6 says, "He that goeth forth and
weepeth, bearing precious seed..." shall what?
"...shall doubtless come again with *rejoicing*, bringing
his sheaves with him." Doubtless means "of a truth,
surely, definitely."

What does this mean? The plowing, planting, and
waiting has meant blood, sweat, and tears for the
Church. But when you get into harvest season, there
is rejoicing, because you bring the sheaves with you.
The sheaves are the fruit, the precious souls —
harvest. When you start seeing people rejoicing,
shouting, laughing, and full of joy, you know we have

stepped over from the *weeping* season to the *rejoicing* season — from a time of planting over into harvest season — and Jesus' return is right around the corner!

Harvest Is Fun!

Plowing and planting is work; but in harvest season, everything changes. There is one set of equipment to plow and plant, but when harvest season comes, there is a whole different set of equipment. Farmers need machines that will bring in the harvest.

God is equipping the Church with new harvest tools: signs, wonders, miracles, and an outpouring of the Holy Ghost. God is getting us ready! We are getting refreshed and full of joy!

What we are seeing now with the refreshing is like a timepiece to show us we are right at the edge of the rain, the harvest, and the return of Jesus. We shouldn't be surprised at Holy Ghost joy-filled meetings like we are experiencing; we should be shocked if we weren't having meetings like these. We can't have them at every service, but we need them at times. *These are times of refreshing!*

I've talked to friends who worked in the wheat fields in Kansas. They prepare ahead of time to get everything ready for the harvest season. When it is time, they turn on the engines and run the equipment 24 hours a day until the harvest is gathered. It took months for the harvest to be ready, but it only takes a few weeks to bring it all in.

God is refreshing us now to go and bring in the harvest. When the latter rain starts falling and the harvest starts coming in, it won't be long before we will be caught up with Jesus in the air!

Chapter 6
Prelude to Revival

We shout at football games, so why shouldn't we shout in church?

We shout when our team is three points ahead, so why shouldn't we shout about how Jesus defeated Satan?

It never bothered me to shout in the world, so why should it bother me to act that way in church? Church services have been dry long enough. It's about time the church had some life in it!

If we were just having meetings where people get drunk in the Holy Ghost and laughed and rejoiced, it would still be enjoyable; but God is doing more than that — He's getting us full of His Spirit!

And there is more going on *inside* us than what people see happening on the outside. In fact, what is seen on the outside is only the effect of what is happening within us.

We should not go to Holy Ghost meetings simply to experience a feeling — to laugh, dance, or feel drunk in the Holy Ghost. We should go for the *cause* of this joy, not these effects.

Our intention should be to get filled to overflowing with God. Then the outward effects will be additional benefits. This overflow into believers' lives is a work of the Holy Ghost, the Comforter whom Jesus promised would come.

Another Comforter

Jesus said in John 14:16, "And I will pray the Father, and he shall give you another Comforter, that he may abide with you for ever...." Notice that Jesus didn't say, "A Comforter"; He said, *"another* Comforter." Jesus seemed to put the Holy Ghost on the same level of importance as Himself.

In John 16:7, He said, "Nevertheless I tell you the truth; It is expedient for you that I go away: for if I go not away, the Comforter will not come unto you; but if I depart, I will send him unto you."

For three and a half years the disciples had been walking and talking with Jesus, sitting at His feet, watching Him perform miracles. They saw Him turn water into wine, feed the multitudes, heal the sick, cleanse the lepers, raise the dead, and cast out devils. Then, after three and a half years, He told them, "I'm going to leave, but it will be *better* for you."

They probably replied, "There's no way it could *ever* be better than this!"

But Jesus insisted it would be *profitable* for them if He left. How could that be? Because the One who anointed Him to do miracles, signs and wonders would now be *in* them instead of simply *with* them.

Jesus was saying, "What I've done for you, the Holy Ghost will do for you. I taught you until this time; now He will teach you. I have healed you until this time; now He will heal you. I have met your needs until this time; now He will meet your needs. The Comforter is the One who will deliver to you whatever I purchase through my death, burial, and resurrection."

An Amazing Conductor

A power station outside the city produces the power that we need to use lights, appliances, sound systems, computers, and so forth. But we have to have something to bring the power from the station to us. We need a *conductor*.

Jesus, through His death, burial, and resurrection, bought our redemption, purchased our freedom from sin, made us able to become new creatures in Christ, purchased all things that pertain to life and godliness, and then went to the Father's right hand.

Jesus has everything that belongs to us. We need what He has, but we also need to be able to receive what He has for us. Jesus told His disciples that He would pray to the Father and He would send "another Comforter" — the Holy Ghost. He's the delivery part of the Trinity. That's why the Holy Ghost is so important: He delivers everything Jesus bought and paid for with His own precious blood.

John 16:7 in *The Amplified Bible* says the word "Comforter" means Counselor, Helper, Advocate, Intercessor, Strengthener, and Standby. If you need a comforter, He's in you. If you need a counselor, He's in you. If you need help, the Helper is in you. He knows *everything* — the past, the present and the future. He knows the end from the beginning. He knows our future better than we know our past or present.

In the Book of Acts, God shows us that if He can get His people filled with the Holy Ghost, all the benefits He brings will be manifested much easier.

If God can get us overflowing with the Holy Ghost it will be far easier for Him to comfort us, heal us, deliver us, and set us free.

If God can get us filled with the Holy Ghost as He did on the Day of Pentecost, everything He has is going to start working in a greater measure in and through us from the inside out.

A Drastic Change

The Holy Ghost wants to change people's lives. We saw an example of a dramatic change in someone's life in one of our meetings. In that series of meetings, we first ministered on joy. Then we began to see the move of the Holy Ghost in an unusual way.

At the end of the meeting, I told the congregation, "We will lay hands on anyone who wants a fresh refilling and trust God to fill you." As we began to lay hands on people, a young woman fell to the floor and lay there the rest of the evening. In fact, she was still there when we left the building.

The next night when I was teaching, I heard a commotion. This same woman had fallen out of her chair again and lay on the floor for the rest of the meeting. The third night, right in the middle of the service, this same woman wrapped her arm around another woman's neck and was helped out of the sanctuary.

The next morning she saw me after the service and said, "I need to talk to you. I've been here all three services. I'm not normally like this. You can ask the pastor. I'm a problem in the church. The pastor and his wife have been kind to me. They have counseled and shared the Word with me for years. I've needed help.

Resurrected From a Living Death

"About 13 years ago, a tragedy came into my home. When this happened, I died inside. For the last 13 years, I've been a walking corpse and worthless to my family. But I got in that line the first night, and before you could even get to me to pray, the power of God fell on me, and I lay on the floor the rest of the evening.

"When I finally got up, my back was completely healed. I'd had severe lower back problems for years. I've not had a pain since then. I was instantly healed.

"I came back the next night, and before I knew it, I was on the floor drunk in the Holy Ghost. The next night, that same presence came on me. I really wanted to know what was happening in these services, so I asked the woman next to me if she would help me outside. I thought if I could get some fresh air, I would be okay, but it didn't work.

"I was drunk in the Holy Ghost three nights in a row. In the last three days, God has turned me around on the inside. I'm alive for the first time in years. I'm not a walking corpse anymore.

A Strange Sound

"At 5 o'clock this morning, I woke myself up laughing hysterically. It was such a strange sound in our house, it woke my husband up. When he looked at me, the laughter jumped off me and landed on him, and he started laughing hysterically, too. We were lying in bed at 5 o'clock in the morning laughing hysterically.

"That sound has not been in our home for 13 years. Now there is joy in our home, joy in me, and joy in my husband. I received a dose of the Holy Ghost, and He has changed me!"

The next night, I announced to the congregation, "We have not had a healing service or even laid hands on the sick, because we were endeavoring to get you full of the Holy Ghost. One woman has already been healed. Is there anyone else who has been healed this week?" Hands went up all over the congregation.

The Deliverer of Healing

We had more people healed in those meetings than we ever had healed in the healing services! Why? *The Holy Ghost delivers the healing.* The more we get of Him, the easier it is to receive what He has for us!

We were in another meeting, laying hands on people, and I noticed a woman who walked with an aluminum cane. Instantly, she handed that cane to someone and took off running around the church auditorium.

When we returned to that church a few months later, she greeted us at the door. She said, "I want you to know I had an accident about four years ago and the doctors told me I would never live a day in my life without pain or walk without that cane. But the power of God fell on me, and I got a good dose of the Spirit of God.

"Before I knew it, I handed my cane to someone and took off running. I want you to know there's not a pain in my body; I am perfectly healed, and I'm staying that way!"

People have been healed of all kinds of sicknesses and diseases in these Holy Ghost services.

Holy Ghost Witnessing

We heard another testimony from a man who came into a meeting and encountered the power of God like never before. The next day at work while he was stacking boxes, the power of God came on him again, and he began to get drunk in the Holy Ghost. Finally he went to his boss and said, "I have to go home."

The boss said, "You look drunk."

He said, "I am."

The boss said, "But I know you. You don't drink."

He said, "I haven't had anything to drink."

"Well, what in the world is going on?"

The man said, "Something happened to me at church. For some reason, whatever I experienced during that meeting is still on me."

The next Sunday, three of his co-workers came to his church to find out what he received because they wanted a dose of it!

Notable Miracles

We were at a church in another state, holding Friday night, Saturday night, and Sunday morning services, and we met a 17-year-old boy who had taken some LSD and lost his mind a few months before.

The doctor told his parents, "There's a 50:50 chance that his mind will come back." So the parents went to the pastor and asked him to agree with them for healing and for their son's mind to be restored. When it was restored, the first thing the boy did was go to church and get right with God. He's been like a fireball for God ever since.

He started to bring his friends in off the streets to our meetings. You would think that these young men may have been offended, but all of them got in the prayer line and said, "I want some of that. That is better than what I've been taking!"

So we started laying hands on the young men, and the power of God fell on them, and they fell to the floor and got up later, drunk in the Holy Ghost. Then they said, "I want another dose!" I invited them to get in line as often as they wanted, because I wanted them to get as full of the Holy Ghost as they could!

The next night, a different group of young men came in. On Sunday morning, still another group came to the meeting. The pastor told us, "In those three services, 14 of the young people were born again, and nine were baptized with the Holy Ghost. What you didn't know was that almost every one of them was a drug addict. God instantly delivered every one of them."

Filled to Overflowing

What were we doing? Just laying hands on people and letting God fill them up. One dose of the Holy Ghost can do more in three minutes than we can do in three years using man's methods.

Some people say, "This is ridiculous — people laughing and getting drunk in the Holy Ghost!" No, *it's the Holy Ghost doing a work on the inside.* Although it shows up on the outside, what's showing up on the outside is the result of what is taking place on the inside.

As the rain that will bring in the harvest begins to fall, God wants to fill us to overflowing.

Many of us have been in trouble because our "fuel tanks" have been empty, and we've been taking in all this "dirt" from the world. God is filling us up!

When we get filled on the inside, there will be no room for problems that have been dominating us.

When we get good and full of the Holy Ghost, we won't need help from others; we will be out helping everyone else.

When we get a good dose of the Spirit of God, it will change the whole course and direction of our lives.

The Fresh Anointing

So God is refreshing His Church, and He is unleashing His Holy Ghost refining fire.

I am enjoying the fresh anointing that is flowing through the Church. If it was not more than that, it would be great; however, there is a deep move of the Holy Ghost that is happening at the same time.

We are beginning to see that when the glory falls on and saturates the congregation, people are filled with joy; they are healed in their bodies; and they are set free.

God is making spiritual deposits in the lives of His people. His purpose is to fill them up so they can go forward with power to reach the lost. We're getting ready to see the fullness of the rain, incredible miracles, and a great harvest. But in the process, God is allowing His Church to be full of joy and to be refreshed. *This isn't a passing fad; it's the prelude to revival!*

Chapter 7
The Other Side of the Doorway

As we have seen previously, the second chapter of Acts is *the doorway to the early rain*.

Peter said, "...this is *[the beginning]* of what was spoken through the prophet Joel..." (Acts 2:16 *Amp.*). It is the beginning — the doorway.

We need to look on the other side of this doorway and find out the purpose of this move of the Holy Ghost and what comes next. What is this move preparing us for? We've looked at the rain and the harvest previously, so now let's get a little more specific.

To see what is in the future, we must look to the past.

The Blueprint of the Early Rain

If we want to know what's on the other side of this move of joy, laughter, hilarity, and drunkenness, let's go back to the Book of Acts. Acts is a picture or a blueprint of the early rain, and if rain is rain, the latter rain will resemble it. Let's walk through the Book of Acts to see what we should expect on the other side of the doorway.

In Acts 1, we find the Early Church in prayer and supplication. They knew a move was coming. Joel had prophesied about it, and Jesus had told them,

"Go tarry in Jerusalem until you are endued with power from on high."

Although they knew a move was coming, they didn't know what it was supposed to look like. That's why they were in prayer and supplication, and that's what we have been doing for years — praying for the rain.

The Rain Is Falling!

In Acts 2, the rain began to fall. Peter said, "This is the beginning of that." This is basically where we are right now in the latter rain. We have been praying, and now the rain has begun to fall!

And when the early rain began to fall, unusual manifestations and demonstrations of the Holy Ghost began to take place. For example, no one had ever spoken in other tongues before, and no one had ever been drunk in the Holy Ghost before.

Acts 2 marked the beginning of unusual demonstrations.

Jesus had already given the disciples a foretaste of the unusual. For example, in John 9, Jesus had ministered healing in a most unusual manner, healing a man who had been blind from his birth.

JOHN 9:6,7
6 When he had thus spoken, he spat on the ground, and made clay of the spittle, and he anointed the eyes of the blind man with the clay,
7 And said unto him, Go, wash in the pool of Siloam....

In other words, Jesus put mud in the man's eyes!

The Unusual Rocks the Boat

That would rock the boat of some people, and they would say, "I'm never going to go to His meeting again; He's putting mud in people's eyes!" If something brings glory to God, lifts up the Name of Jesus, and brings blessings to mankind, we need to follow it. Just because it's a little *unusual* doesn't mean it's *unscriptural*. Then, in Mark 7, Jesus went into the region of Tyre and Sidon, and the Word says, "They bring unto him one that was deaf, and had an impediment in his speech; and they beseech him to put his hand upon him" (verse 32).

The Bible tells us Jesus took this deaf man and led him aside from the multitude. Then Jesus put His fingers in the man's ears, spit, and touched his tongue.

Can you believe it? Here Jesus is, and they want the laying on of hands — and Jesus spit on the man! In some churches today He would have lost half the congregation at that moment. They would say, "We're not putting up with any of this. We haven't seen it before."

There are many things we haven't seen before, but if we will go back through Church history from the Day of Pentecost to the present, we will find many unusual manifestations of the Holy Ghost.

When Jesus took the deaf man aside from the multitude, put His fingers in his ears, and spit, the man was completely healed!

In Demonstration of the Spirit and of Power

Paul described his own ministry in First Corinthians 2.

1 CORINTHIANS 2:1-5
1 And I, brethren, when I came to you, came not with excellency of speech or of wisdom, declaring unto you the testimony of God.
2 For I determined not to know any thing among you, save Jesus Christ, and him crucified.
3 And I was with you in weakness, and in fear, and in much trembling.
4 And my speech and my preaching was not with enticing words of man's wisdom, but in demonstration of the Spirit and of power:
5 That your faith should not stand in the wisdom of men, but in the power of God.

Paul said, "I came to you with teaching, preaching, and demonstration of the Spirit." He didn't explain every demonstration of the Spirit that happened, but we know the demonstrations brought glory to God, blessings to man, and lifted up the Name of Jesus.

The Gospel writers didn't list *everything* that happened in Jesus' ministry, either. At the end of the Book of John, writing of Jesus, John said:

JOHN 21:25
25 And there are also MANY OTHER THINGS which Jesus did, the which, if they should be written every one, I suppose that even the world itself could not contain the books that should be written.

So we don't have a complete list of everything Jesus said and did on Earth; we only have certain incidents described in a condensed form.

MATTHEW 14:35,36
35 And when the men of that place [Gennesaret] **had knowledge of him, they sent out into**

**all that country round about, and brought
unto him all that were diseased;
36 And besought him that they might only
touch the hem of his garment: and as many as
touched were made perfectly whole.**

In other words, sometimes so many miracles
happened so fast, no one could write them down!

Something Unusual

As long as manifestations of the Holy Ghost bless
mankind, give glory to God, and are not contrary to
the Word, let's not throw them out until we see what
kind of fruit results.

We were recently in a meeting where a woman
said, "I can't move my feet!" She was frozen. After a
while we took a chair to her so she could sit down.
But she couldn't bend her legs to sit in the chair. She
was glued to the floor! Unusual? Yes!

As the glory began to lift, she fell under the
power of God and lay there, shaking, for 15 to 20
minutes. When we finally left, she was sitting in a
chair with her hands lifted toward heaven — frozen
again! Not only did she experience an unusual
encounter with the Holy Ghost, but God also used it
as a demonstration of His presence to the congregation.

On another occasion following an evening
meeting, we noticed the youth pastor lying on the
floor in the middle of the fellowship hall, staring at
the ceiling.

The pastor said, "I don't know where he is, but I
want to be the first to talk to him when he gets

back!" We watched him for 45 minutes, and he never moved a muscle or blinked an eye. He just stared at the ceiling in a trance. Unusual.

All of a sudden, we saw a couple of his fingers move. The pastor walked over to him and asked, "Are you back?"

He said, "Oh, pastor, I'm glad to see you. Suddenly it was as if the whole ceiling disappeared, and all I could see were glistening clouds of glory. I knew that just over on the other side of those clouds was heaven. I've been lying here enjoying myself."

God manifested Himself in an unusual way, and it sparked a greater move of God in that youth department.

So we are coming into some unusual demon-strations: manifestations of trances, manifestations of visions, and manifestations of angels. In recent times, there have been two instances of young people experiencing visions of heaven. While under the power of God, Jesus appeared to them and escorted them through heaven.

God is in the "sign" business! We may as well get ready for the unusual, because if it happened in the Book of Acts, we're going to have it today.

Struck Dumb

In the Old Testament, the prophet Ezekiel sat down by the river Chebar and remained there "astonished" (or amazed) for seven days (Ezekiel 3:14,15). One meaning of the word "astonished" is "to be struck dumb" or "to be dumb."

Another reference to being struck dumb is found in Ezekiel 33.

EZEKIEL 33:22
22 Now the hand of the Lord was upon me in the evening, afore he that was escaped came; and had opened my mouth, until he came to me in the morning; and my mouth was opened, and I WAS NO MORE DUMB.

"What about examples in the New Testament?" some will ask. What about John the Baptist's father, Zacharias?

The angel of the Lord came to him and announced, "You are going to have a son."

Zacharias replied, "How do I know this is true? Give me a sign."

The angel said, "I'll give you a sign." Zacharias was struck dumb, and he could not speak until the child was born. Unusual things.

We are on the edge of some very unusual manifestations and demonstrations of the Spirit of God.

A Great Flow of Divine Healing

As the Church stepped from Acts 2 to Acts 3, great manifestations of divine healing emerged. Peter and John, on their way to the Temple at the hour of prayer, saw a crippled man asking for alms at the Gate Beautiful. Peter, "fastening his eyes upon him," said, "Look on us...Silver and gold have I none; but such as I have give I thee: In the name of Jesus Christ of Nazareth rise up and walk" (Acts 3:4,6).

If a great flow of divine healing and strong manifestations of gifts of healings happened right after
the doorway of the early rain, we can probably
expect the same things to happen right after we step
through the doorway of the latter rain.

The disciples saw 3000 people get saved through
the *joy* of the Day of Pentecost in Acts 2, yet one
miraculous *healing* described in Acts 3 drew such a
crowd that 5000 men came to the Lord.

The sudden realization of what could be accomplished through signs, wonders, and healings,
caused the Early Church to step into Acts 4.

Finding Your Own Company

After the crippled man at the Gate Beautiful was
raised up, Peter and John were commanded by the
authorities not to preach or teach any more in the
Name of Jesus. They returned, Acts 4:23 reports, to
"their own company."

This is important. There seemed to be a real
emphasis on finding their own company. Peter and
John knew their own company, and when they got in
trouble, they returned to that company. They knew
those people would stand with them. The Bible says:

> **ACTS 4:24**
> **24 And when they heard that, they lifted up
> their voice to God with one accord and said,
> Lord, thou art God which hast made heaven,
> and earth, and the sea, and all that in them is.**

Notice the first thing they did was to praise God.
As we look on the other side of the door, we see a

renewed emphasis on prayer, praise, and worship.
Ministering to the Lord is what opens the door for
the presence of God to come and accomplish what
He wants done.

Following a time of praising God, notice the Early
Church began to pray:

> **ACTS 4:29,30**
> **29 And now, Lord, behold their threatenings:
> and grant unto thy servants, that with all
> boldness they may speak thy word,
> 30 By stretching forth thine hand to heal; and
> that SIGNS AND WONDERS may be done by
> the name of thy holy child Jesus.**

They lifted up their voices to God and prayed for
healings, signs, and wonders. The next thing that
happened was the Church discovered the power of
united and corporate prayer.

Liberality in Giving

Also, in Acts 4:34,35, you will notice there was
real liberality in their giving, and prosperity began
to flow into the Church.

> **ACTS 4:34,35**
> **34 NEITHER WAS THERE ANY AMONG THEM
> THAT LACKED: for as many as were posses-
> sors of lands or houses sold them, and brought
> the prices of the things that were sold,
> 35 And laid them down at the apostles' feet:
> and distribution was made unto every man
> according as he had need.**

People began giving to the kingdom of God, the
work of the ministry, and none of them lacked. In

the middle of a move of God or an outpouring of the Holy Ghost, the Church became givers, and everyone prospered.

An Outpouring of the Power Gifts

As a result of the prayers in Acts 4, the Church moved into Acts 5, where we find a manifestation of signs and wonders done through the hands of the apostles. There was a great outpouring of the power gifts of the Spirit. We find that the working of miracles, special faith, and gifts of healings flowed throughout the remainder of the Book of Acts.

Another important turn of events is found in Acts 6. The apostles were the only ministers available at that time. The Church was so new, there had not yet been time to raise up the other ministry gifts.

The Helps Ministry Emerges

As the Early Church grew and prospered, the apostles' workload also grew. Finally the apostles decided, "It's not right for us to wait on all the tables. We need to be giving ourselves to the ministry of the Word and prayer." So they raised up the deacons, or what we would call the helps ministry.

Those in the helps ministry aren't necessarily called to preach or teach, but they are called by God to be a help in the ministry. Acts 6 shows us the results of the helps ministry stepping fully into place as the Word of God increased and the number of disciples multiplied greatly.

Stephen, a helps minister, was greatly used by God in the Early Church. The Bible says he was a man full of faith and the Holy Ghost who did great signs, wonders, and miracles among the people. So we see laymen were used greatly by God in spiritual gifts, in healings, and in demonstrations of the Spirit.

Then in Acts 8, we see the ministry of the evangelist suddenly emerge with Philip. He not only preached Jesus to the Samaritans; visible miracles occurred in his ministry, according to Acts 8:

ACTS 8:6-8
6 And the people with one accord gave heed unto those things which Philip spake, hearing and seeing the miracles which he did.
7 For unclean spirits, crying with loud voice, came out of many that were possessed with them: and many taken with palsies, and that were lame, were healed.
8 And there was great joy in that city.

So in this eighth chapter of Acts we see the fullness of the evangelist's ministry, and a whole city was touched by the power and the presence of God.

When the rain began to fall and the Church stepped through the door, whole cities came in contact with the presence of God.

A Spectacular Conversion

In Acts 9, we find not only spectacular demonstrations of the Spirit, but spectacular conversions of people in influential places.

One such spectacular conversion happened to Saul of Tarsus, the man who had authority to put

Christians in prison and even kill them! As Saul was traveling to Damascus, suddenly a light brighter than the noonday sun shone from heaven, and a voice said, "Saul, Saul, why persecutest thou me?" (Acts 9:4).

Here was a spectacular conversion and a spectacular demonstration of the Spirit in the life of a person in a highly influential position.

Manifestations of Divine Direction

In Acts 10, we see spectacular leadings. Our main goal is to be led by the Spirit of God, and the primary way God leads is through the inward witness. However, after entering through the doorway, we see spectacular leadings in the lives of the early Christians.

Peter went up on the housetop to pray, and suddenly an angel appeared to him and told him what to do. Then the Spirit of the Lord spoke to Peter and told him to go with the Gentiles who had come from Cornelius' house, seeking him.

Even though we are to be led by the Spirit of God by the inward witness, we find a flood of manifestations of divine direction coming to people in the Book of Acts through angelic appearances, the word of the Lord, the voice of the Spirit, visions, and occasional visitations by Jesus Himself.

Supernatural Deliverance

Then, in Acts 12, we note that when the Church prayed, heaven sent angelic help. Herod had killed

James with a sword, saw that it pleased the people, and put Peter in prison, intending to kill him after Easter — but the Church began to pray instantly and earnestly for his release.

An angel walked through the prison door, a light shown into the place, the angel nudged Peter, told him to put on his shoes and his coat, the prison doors opened before him, and Peter had a tremendous deliverance from what looked like certain death.

Separated Into Their Work

But Acts 13 is what we really want to look for. This seems to be a turning point in the Book of Acts. Acts 2 is the door. Acts 3 is where we see divine healings. Acts 4 is where we see the power of united prayer and liberality in finances in the Church. Acts 5 is the beginning of great signs and wonders. Acts 6 shows the ministry of helps. Acts 7 shows laymen being mightily used of God. Acts 8 is a great thrust of evangelism from one-on-one to the masses, followed in chapters 9 through 12 by supernatural conversions and angelic help.

This leads us to Acts 13, where there was a special prayer meeting of ministers at the church in Antioch. Not only did members of the Church find their own company, but *ministers* found their own company.

They came together not simply for fellowship, activity, or relaxation; they came together to minister to the Lord. An atmosphere such as this is conducive for the Holy Ghost to speak, move, and bring forth the plan of God.

As they ministered to the Lord, the Holy Ghost said to them, "...Separate me Barnabas and Saul for the work whereunto I have called them" (Acts 13:2).

Suddenly, there was a great missionary thrust into the nations of the world which lasted through the remainder of the Book of Acts. Barnabas and Saul went into the work God had called them. What was it? They became apostles to the Gentiles or the nations. The remainder of the Book of Acts deals primarily with world missions.

The Book of Acts describes the nations Paul visited, the individuals who were saved through his ministry, his ministry to the masses, his founding of strong local churches, and the establishment in Acts 19:10 of a foreign Bible school that thrust ministers into the harvest fields of the world.

Walking in the Fullness

The last big thrust in the Book of Acts was people walking in the fullness of their callings, reaching out to the unsaved nations of the world. They went forth in the fullness of spiritual gifts, demonstrations of the Spirit, and demonstrations of power.

The Book of Acts was the early rain. If rain is rain, we should expect all of these past experiences to be our pattern for the days to come.

What is the purpose of the current move of the Holy Ghost? Where does the doorway lead us? A great harvest will be brought in, and churches will thrive, becoming "barns" to contain this harvest. When the harvest is finally complete, Jesus will return, and we will all go home!

If we want to experience the rest of the Book of Acts, we must go through the door. But let's not stop there. Let's keep moving on into the other side, flowing with the Word and the Spirit into the fullness of the rain!

For a complete catalog of books and tape series,
or to receive Mark Brazee Ministries free,
bi-monthly newsletter, please write to:

Mark Brazee Ministries
P. O. Box 1870
Broken Arrow, OK 74013